Pigeon Hill: Then + Now

Pigeon Hill: Then + Now

Jeffrey A. Wolin

Introduction by Keith F. Davis
Afterword by Jean-Louis Poitevin

KEHRER

Twenty years—enough time for a baby to become a man proud of his strength or for a young and attractive woman to become a woman whose face we can read like an open book in which her destiny would be written down. Enough as well for liberty to be turned into prison, or the other way around. Nonetheless, when we look at these pictures, and despite these pivotal events, which are told as briefly as a confession, it is impossible not to feel that the notion of time is in some way biased, even false. In any case it is at least without connection to what is really experienced.

– ***Jean-Louis Poitevin***

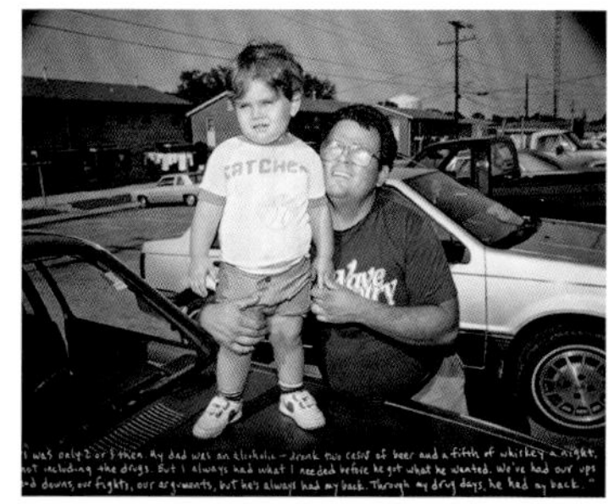

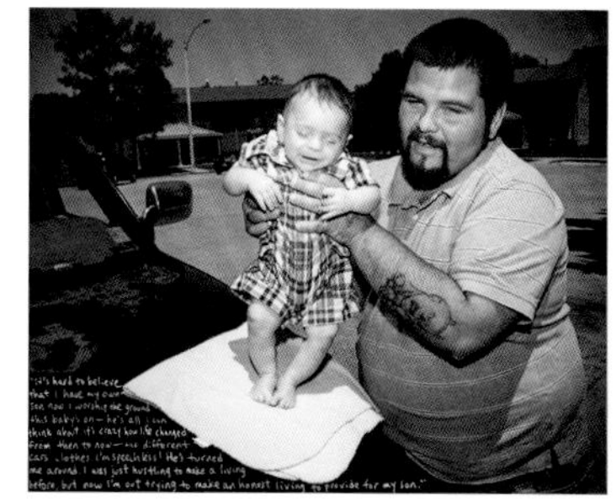

Remarkable for their range and variety, these projects were the result of deep, sustained efforts. Wolin is a patient worker, guided by a clear sense of what he wants to do, but always learning and adapting as he goes. The people and places he cares about are inherently complex. The time required for each project is a clear indication of his fundamental respect for his subjects, for the richness and mystery of the story that demands telling. In part, of course, Wolin's creative patience is a function of his understanding of time and his devotion to the lessons of history.

Introduction

Keith F. Davis

Jeffrey Wolin has produced one of this era's most original and powerful bodies of photographic art. His work is at once poetic and forensic in nature, intuitive and systematic, unflinching yet warmly and deeply human. His photographs embody a continuing meditation on history and the vicissitudes of life. They are about people and time—the texture of lived experience, the relentless trajectory of present into past, and the frail but essential power of memory.

"Wolin strives to honor the full reality of his subjects—the visible aspects of their lives as well as those that can only be imagined; feelings that can be put into words and the realm of the unspoken."

Wolin's vision is a full expression of his own experiences and core concerns. He entered Kenyon College, in Ohio, in 1968, with an inclination toward science, but was soon drawn to the study of English. He wrote poetry and short stories, but gradually found that the camera best satisfied his combined interest in empiricism and creative expression. After a semester's study in Europe, he took classes at the Kalamazoo (Michigan) Institute of Arts while working for two years for that city's police department. This stint as a police photographer was a revelation—it exposed him to a gritty world of "crime and punishment" that he had never seen before. The nature of his duties made him focus on photography's forensic, evidentiary function—the importance of the image as a clear, legally valid representation of *fact*.

In 1974, he began a two-year graduate program at the Rochester Institute of Technology, absorbing the legacy of Minor White and the technical discipline of the large format camera and the Zone System. In addition to his photographic studies, he also continued an earlier interest in letterpress printing and bookmaking. Most important of all, Wolin began working in the photo lab of the George Eastman House in 1976. In addition to overseeing the museum's routine imaging needs, he was immersed in the House's remarkable historical collection. He studied the work—and made prints from vintage negatives—of calotypist John Shaw Smith, the early-twentieth-century Pictorialist Alvin Langdon Coburn, the great social documentarian Lewis Hine, and many others. Through this work and his friendships with figures as varied as the acclaimed modernist, André Kertész, and the 19th century process historian James Reilly, Wolin came to a rich understanding of both personal style and the expressive language of photographic materials.

In this period, Wolin photographed trees in urban settings, in conscious homage to Eugène Atget, the great documentary photographer known for his poetic images of early-twentieth-century Paris. Wolin used a tripod-mounted 8x10-inch camera and made contact prints on Kodak Studio Proof paper using the printing-out method. He loved this work—both the majesty and variety of his subjects and the time-honored simplicity of his technical means.

A born teacher—articulate, knowledgeable, and generous—Wolin served as an adjunct instructor at the University of Rochester in his last two years in the city. In 1980, he accepted a teaching position at Indiana University, Bloomington, beginning a prestigious thirty-year career there that would see him advancing to full professor, director of the School of Fine Arts, and, finally, the honor of an endowed chair. It was in this context, in his first decade in Bloomington, that Wolin came to maturity as a creative artist.

Wolin's first photographic project in Indiana was an immediate response to the area's landscape and economy. He was fascinated by the many limestone quarries near Bloomington and the fact that local stone had gone into such iconic structures as the Empire State Building, the Pentagon, Rockefeller Center, Grand Central Station, New York's Metropolitan Museum of Art, and innumerable other cultural landmarks. Several years of intense effort resulted in the book *Stone Country* (Indiana University Press, 1985), with Wolin's photographs and a text by Scott R. Sanders, a professor of English at the university.

Even while completing *Stone Country*, Wolin was already exploring a variety of other subjects. With a hand-held medium-format camera, he began photographing in Bloomington's impoverished Pigeon Hill neighborhood. Working intermittently over a period of several years, Wolin talked to residents and made portraits, exploring in a general way the effect of the environment on those who lived there. As a matter of creative affinity, in thinking about his own formative environment, he began his "Autobiography" series, centering on images of his aging mother and father, as well as key life experiences. This consideration of his immediate family led to larger thoughts about identity, community, and the legacy of the Holocaust. With his 8x10 camera in Paris, in 1981, he began what would turn into a nearly two-decade long meditation on the survivors of the Nazi death camps.

This overlapping of photographic projects was at once stimulating and daunting, rich with possibilities but without any easy or obvious resolution. The problem, in part, was that each project pointed beyond the exclusive realm of the visual. For Wolin, the making of these images stemmed from a complex process of interaction and learning, extended and often deeply personal conversations, and much thinking about culture and history. As a result, it seemed that *something else*, some other expressive form or tool, was required to do these projects appropriate artistic justice.

Thus, it was altogether appropriate that the *Stone Country* collaboration renewed Wolin's interest in writing and in the integration of words and pictures. This idea was further stimulated by a folk art exhibition at the Indiana University School of Fine Arts Gallery, with painting-text works by Howard Finster and Sister Gertrude Morgan, and by Wolin's consideration of other historical precedents, from medieval illuminated manuscripts to the work of twentieth-century artists such as Frieda Kahlo and Duane Michals.

The result was a deliberate and dramatic change in his working method. Turning from the apparent "objectivity" of a classical documentary mode, Wolin began adding hand-written texts to the surface of his prints. This autographic intervention went against much of what he admired in the history of photographic practice, but it felt both *right* and *necessary* to his creative intentions. He had long recognized—and valued—the fact that words and pictures work in different ways. Now, he brought those distinct strengths together, exploring their potential in combination.

The strength of this approach was at least two-fold. First, Wolin's idea was distinctly daring—filling 16x20-inch photographic prints with dense and lengthy texts, in order to make *looking* and *reading* genuinely intertwined, mutually informing activities. Second, Wolin succeeded where others have failed in combining words and pictures due, in large measure, to the quality of his writing. Notably, his text and images reflect a consistent level of expressive craft, the same degree of care, precision, and emotional investment.

The first piece realized in this new mode was *My Father*, 1985, in which fully two-thirds of the image area is filled with a hand-scripted narrative of the hard life and physical decline of an honest, ordinary man. This was a key work in Wolin's "Autobiography" series (1985–1992), which also included image-text pieces dedicated to his mother, Wolin's friendship with André Kertész, and his work as a police photographer. Greeted warmly by curators such as Peter Galassi of the Museum of Modern Art, this series put Wolin firmly on the artistic map.

He used a similar image-text approach for his subsequent series "Pigeon Hill" (1987–1991), and "Written in Memory: Portraits of the Holocaust" (1992–1996). In his "Life at the Millennium: Family Photographs" series (beginning 1996), Wolin modified this approach by having his children write their own commentary on his images of them. Taking a deliberate break from the emotional intensity of his Holocaust effort, his "Ancient Provence" series (2000–2003) uses straightforward images, without text, to suggest the enduring presence of the Roman past in the south of France. Wolin modified his image-text presentation yet again in another large and emotionally draining project, portraits of Vietnam War veterans from both sides of the conflict (2003–2010). This work continues the synergy of images and words, but the narrative texts are adjacent to, rather than inscribed on, the photographs. Remarkable for their range and variety, these projects were the result of deep, sustained efforts. Wolin is a patient worker, guided by a clear sense of what he wants to do, but always learning and adapting as he goes. The people and places he cares about are inherently complex. The time required for each project is a clear indication of his fundamental respect for his subjects, for the richness and mystery of the story that demands telling. In part, of course, Wolin's creative patience is a function of his understanding of time and his devotion to the lessons of history. History informs everything; the present is a product of the past and an intimation of the future. Time moves slowly but inexorably; it is relentless, an agent of both renewal and annihilation. This is the key theme of Wolin's life's work—an elegant, poignant, and ultimately universal meditation on temporality and memory.

"These images engage a sense of 'destiny'—the idea that personality and fate are shaped early in life."

These qualities are exemplified in the work encompassed in *Pigeon Hill: Then & Now*—Wolin's return to a place, and lives, that he first explored a generation ago. This renewed attention speaks to his guiding concerns; the quality of this work demonstrates his special artistic insight. These pictures are surprising, poignant, tragic, and heroic. Above all, they are vital; they convey the reality, the grit and texture, of life. These images engage a sense of "destiny"—the idea that personality and fate are shaped early in life. However, they also make clear that few things are truly predestined; we all grow and change, just as we are all a product of chance and contingency. This complexity is underscored by Wolin's brilliant orchestration of visual information—the telling details of expression, gesture, and environment that suggest an intimate sense of actual lives rooted in a particular time and place.

Wolin's texts add another dimension of specificity of the images. He deals with artful slices of reality: the photographs are carefully composed vignettes of experience, each reflecting a fraction of a second of lived time; the words are potent distillations of a much larger process of engagement and conversation. Thus, Wolin presents us with his understanding of a "decisive moment" of perception joined to, and amplified by, a poetically concise verbal reflection or thought. And, of course, this result is amplified yet again by his pairings, the remarkable leap in time between "then" and "now."

The result of this artistic synthesis is at once radiantly clear and endlessly mysterious. This tension is entirely intentional. Wolin strives to honor the full reality of his subjects—the visible aspects of their lives as well as those that can only be imagined; feelings that can be put into words and the realm of the unspoken. Consequently, he never pretends to "explain" the people he records. Instead, he presents compelling evidence of their physical and mental lives, with the full knowledge that the integrity of a life always defies easy reduction or summary. None of these lives is generic or simple. Walt Whitman famously proclaimed: "I am large, I contain multitudes." It is Wolin's gift to so clearly suggest not only the journey—the pathos, the effort, and the insight—of everyday life, but the multitudes that dwell within us all.

Keith F. Davis
Senior Curator of Photography
Nelson-Atkins Museum of Art

THEN

Photographs 1987–1991

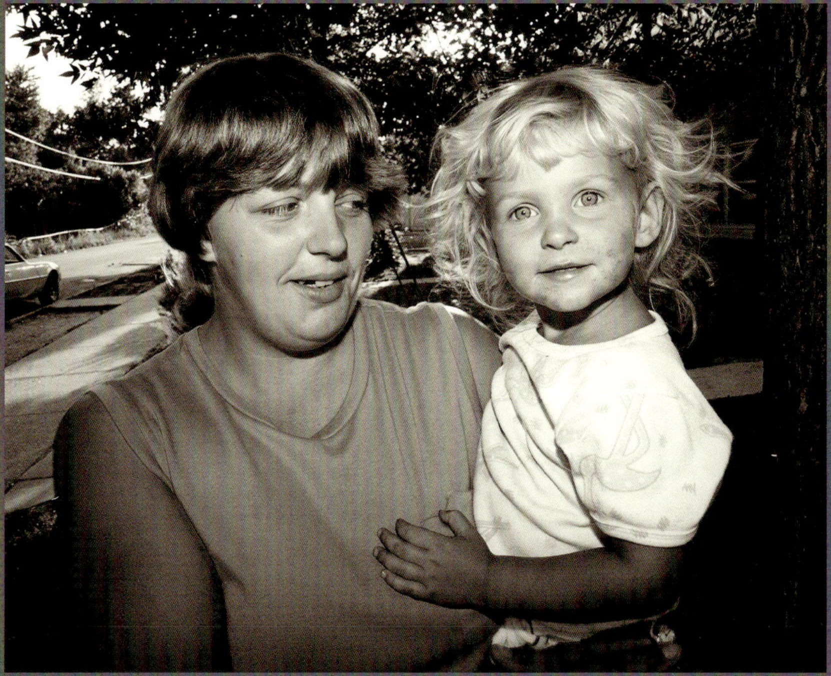

In this suite of images I wanted to show the range of experiences I encountered in the housing projects from the destructive to the joyful. As I observed and photographed some of the problems associated with life in the housing projects—violence, drug and alcohol abuse, truancy, teen pregnancy, child abuse—I focused on something else as well: a strong and diverse community where kids had shoals of other kids to play with and families with deep, lasting bonds. Most of the individuals who appear in the following grids can be found later in the "Now" section grids as well, unless they died or otherwise couldn't be found.

*– **Jeffrey A. Wolin***

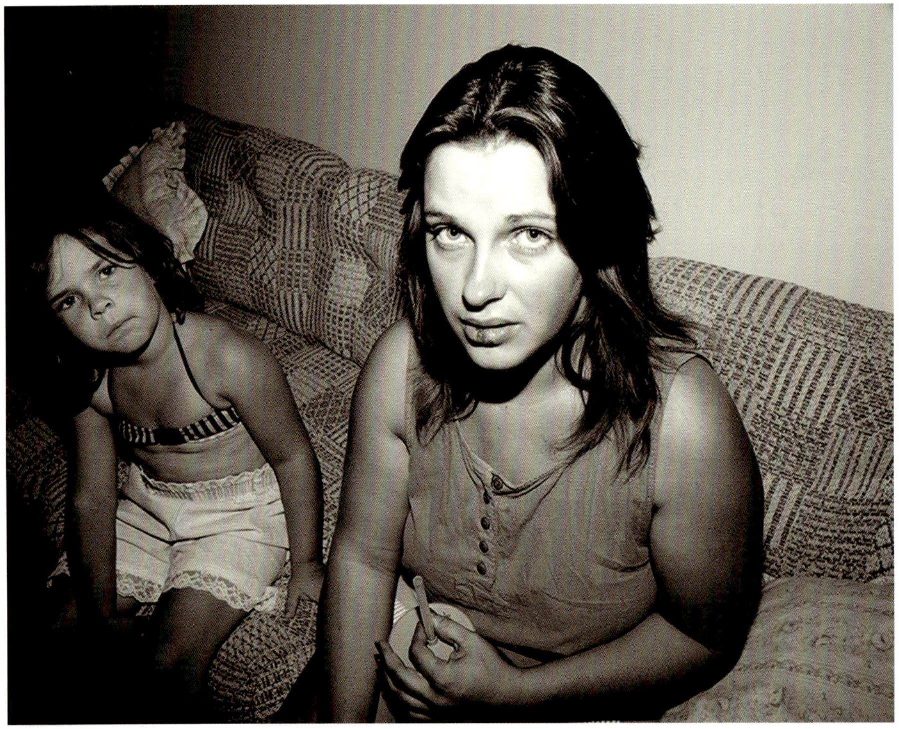
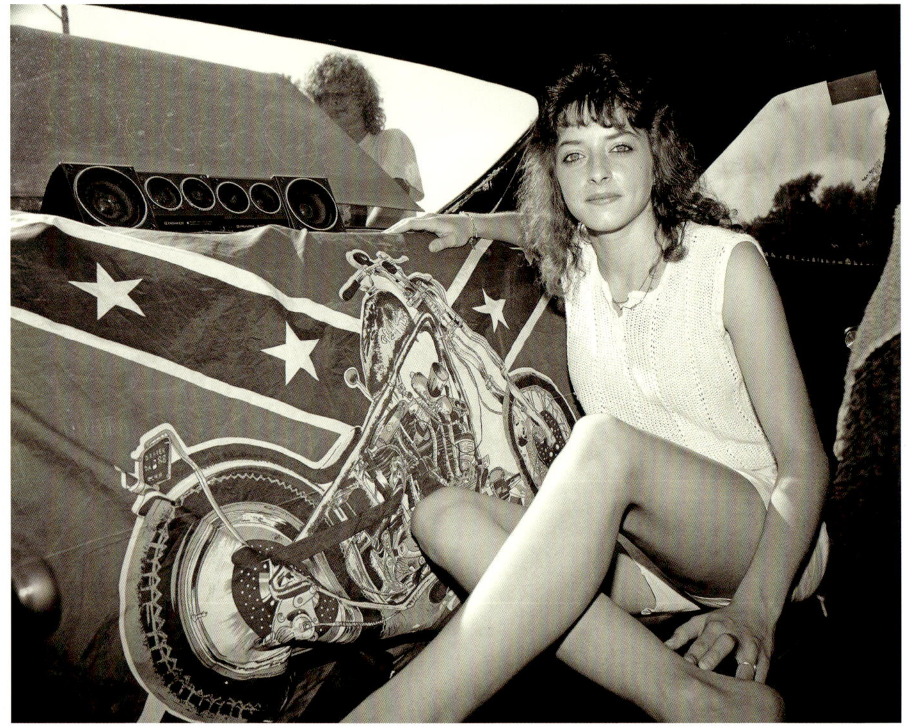
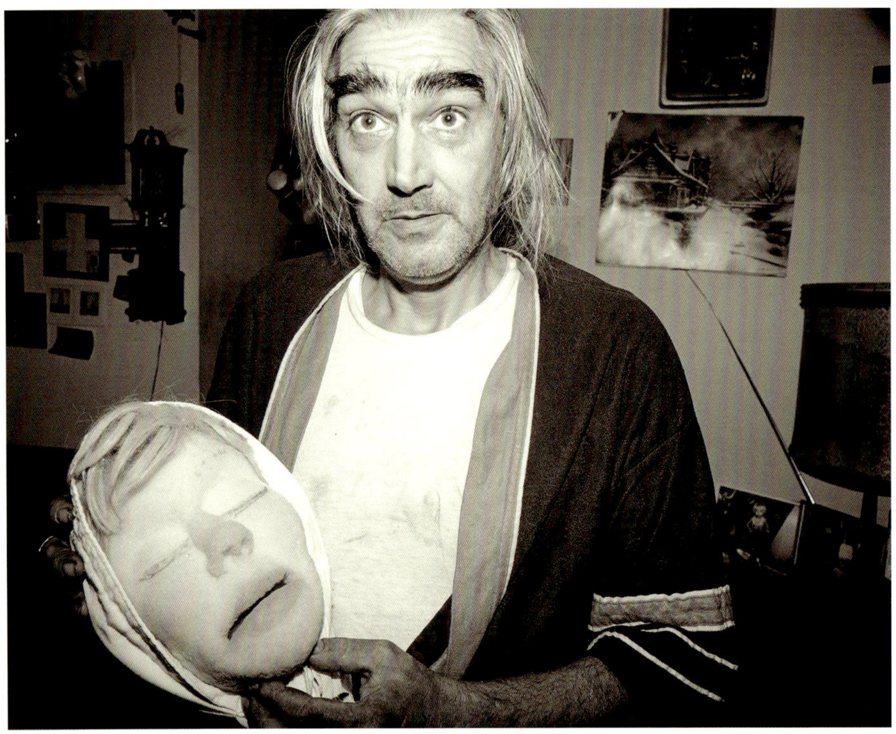
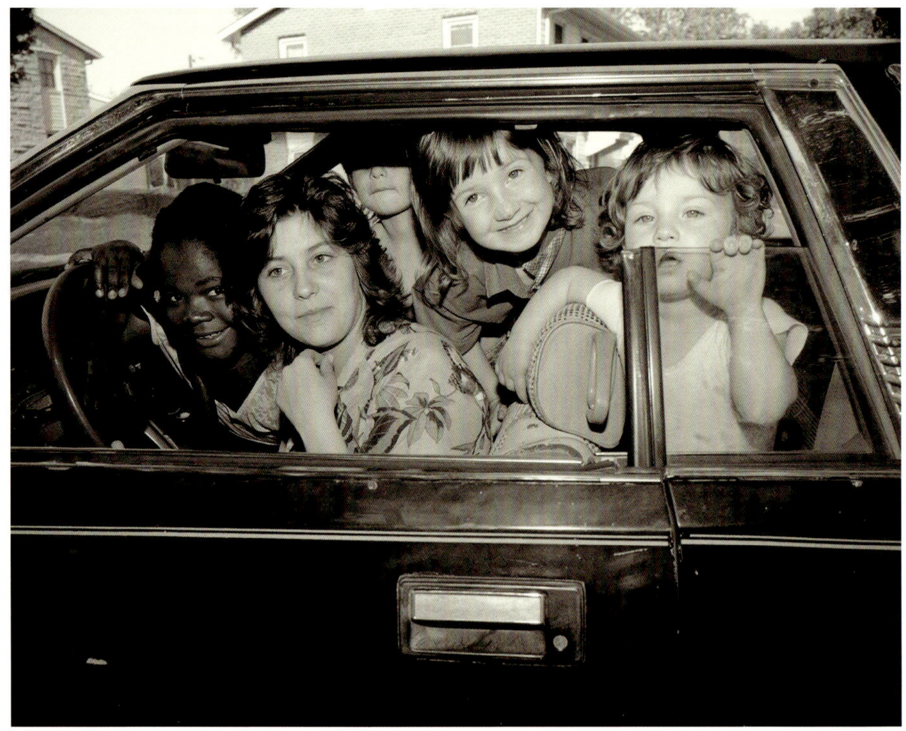

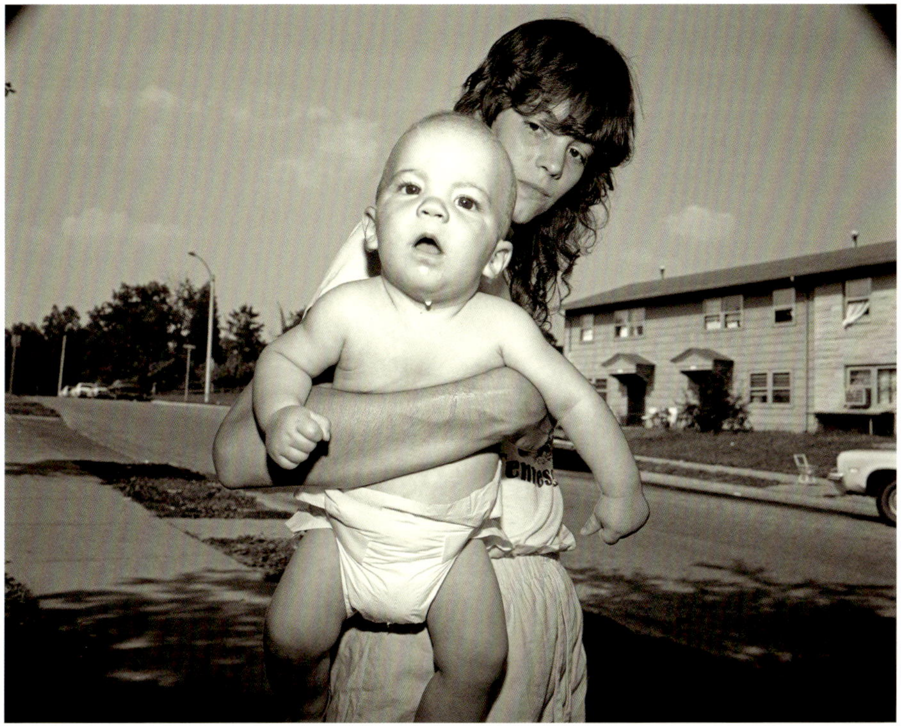

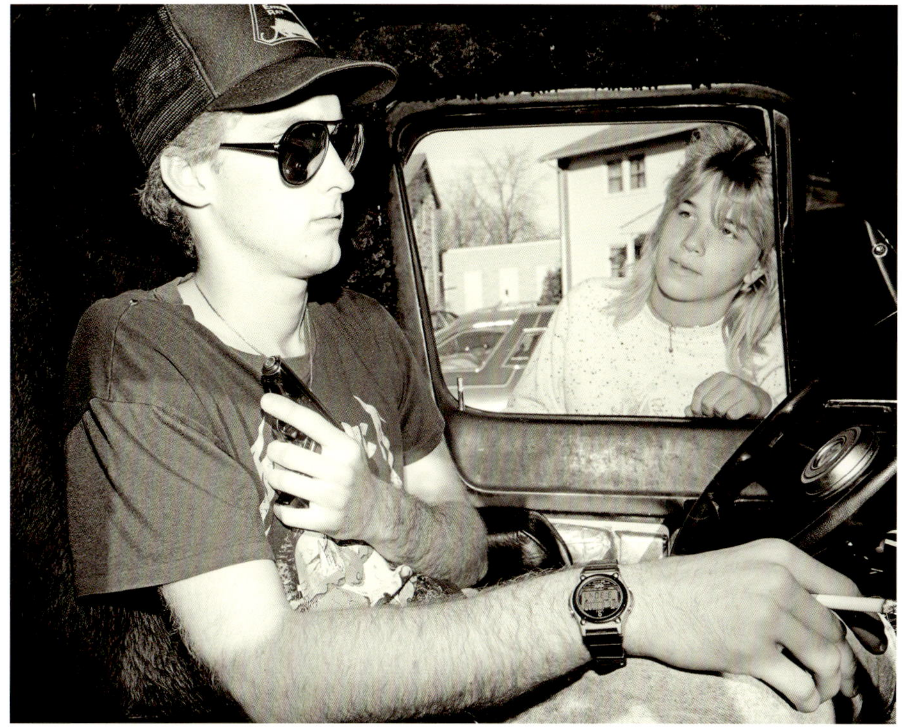

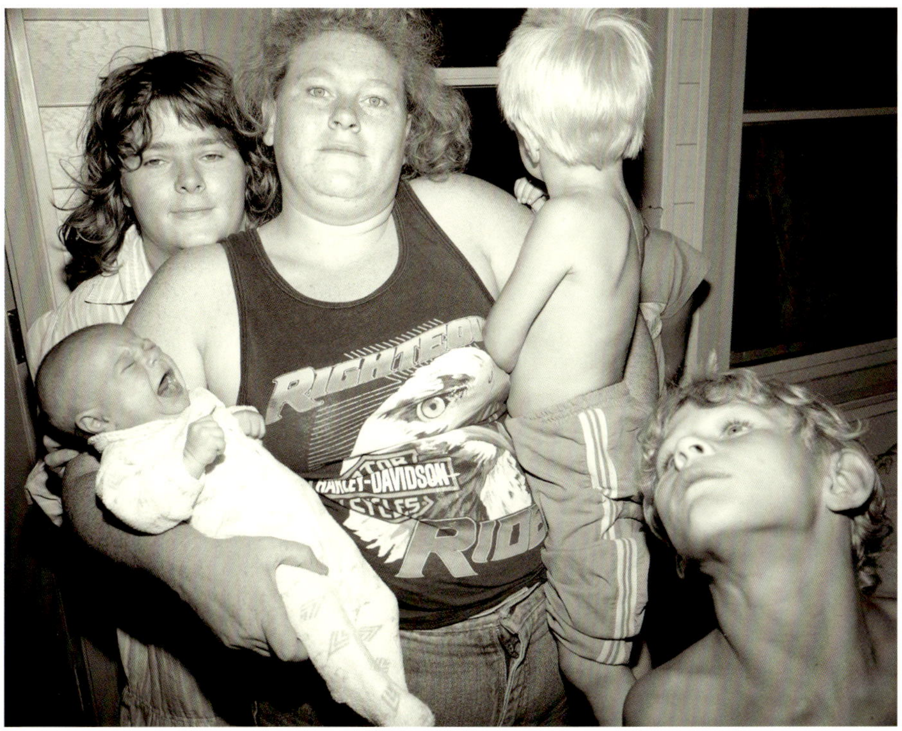
HARLEY-DAVIDSON

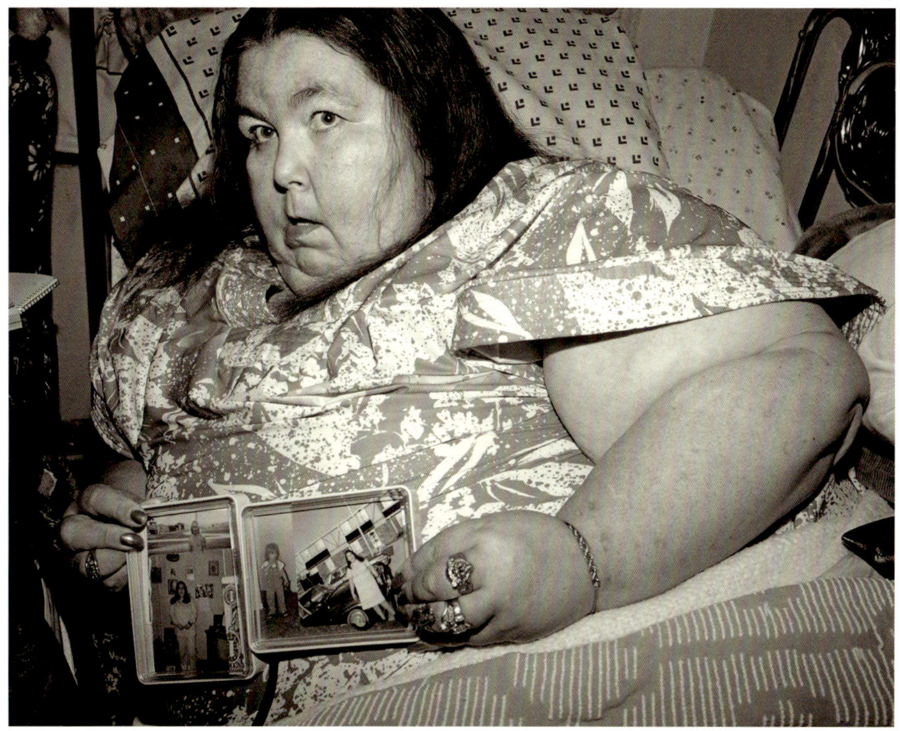

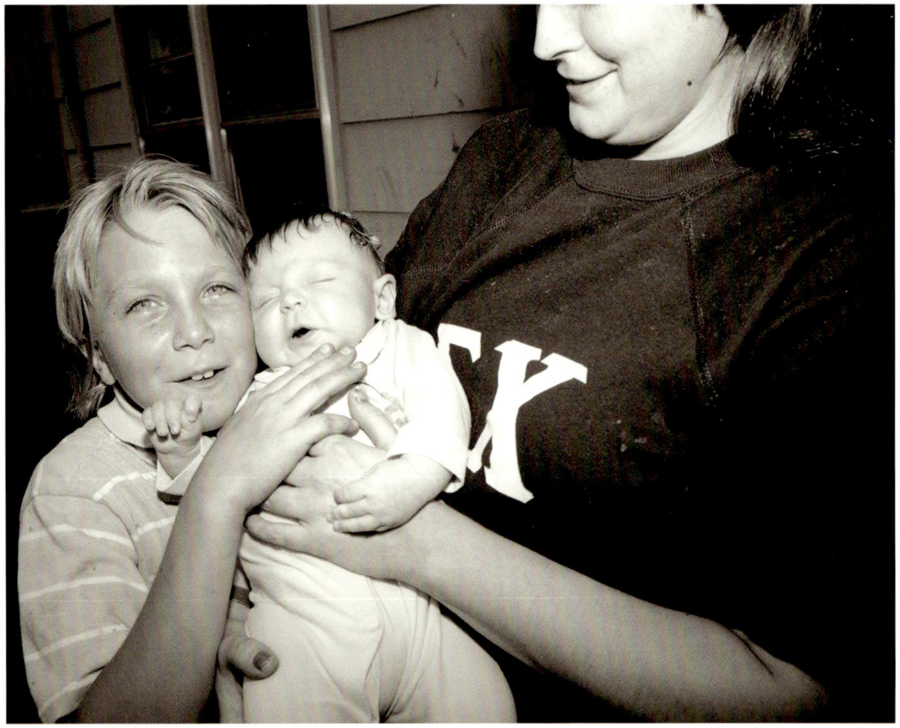

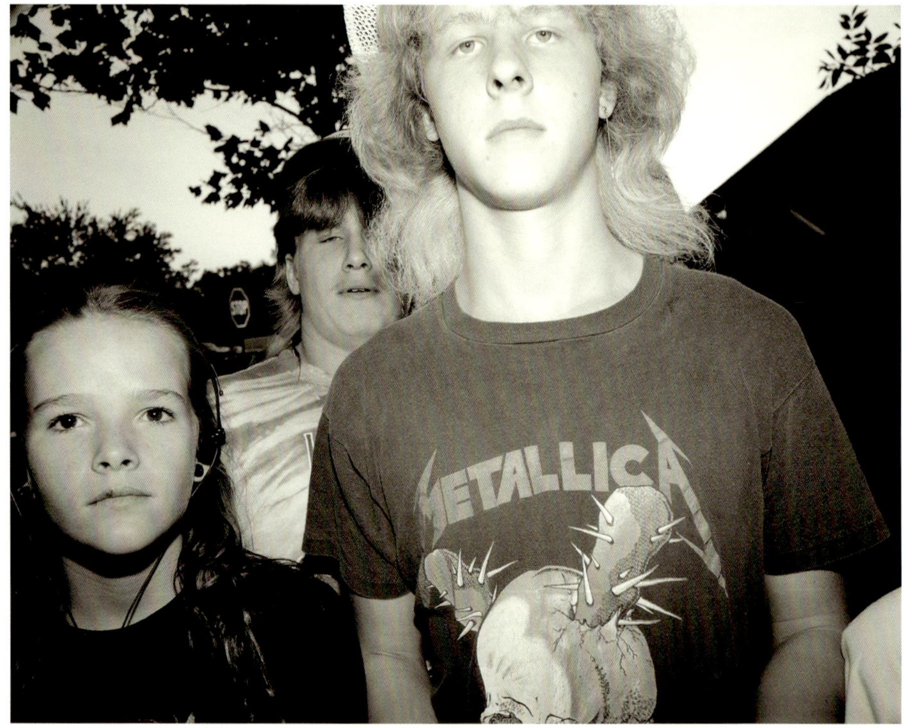
METALLICA

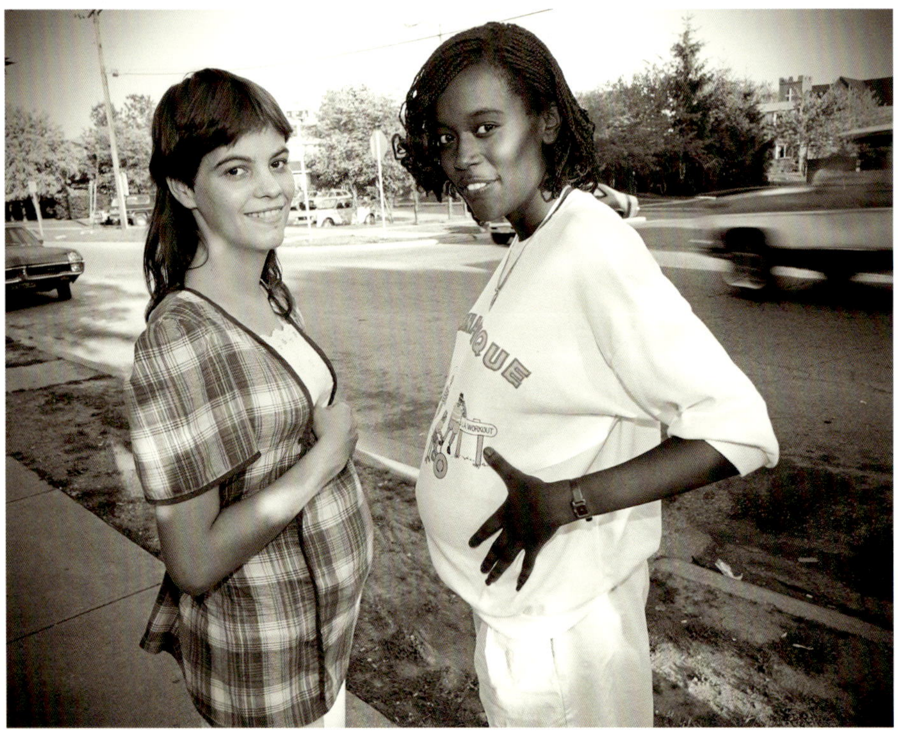

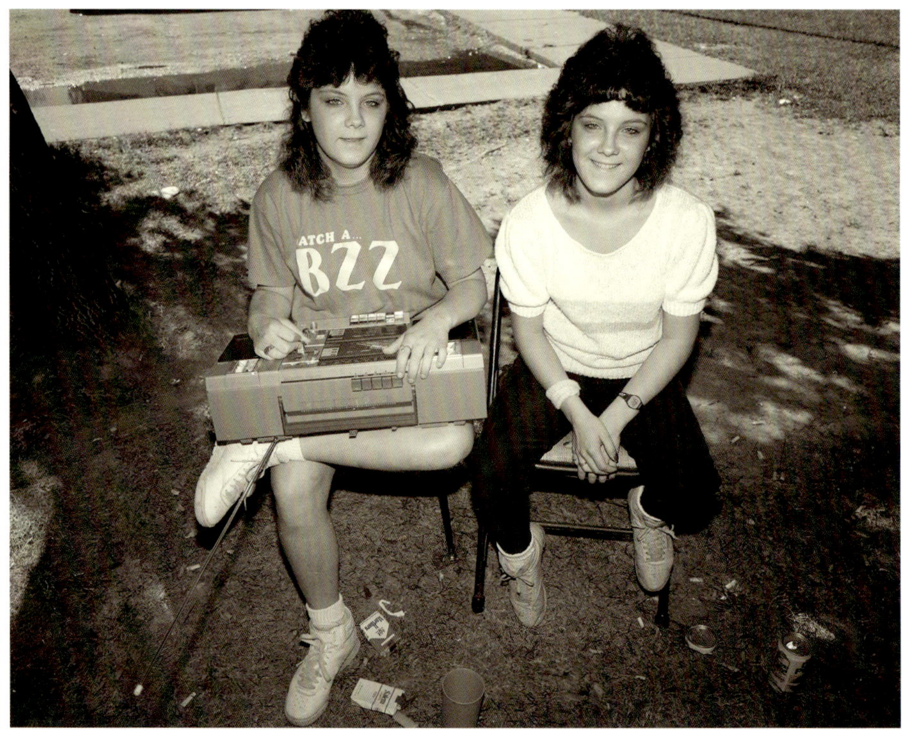
BZZ

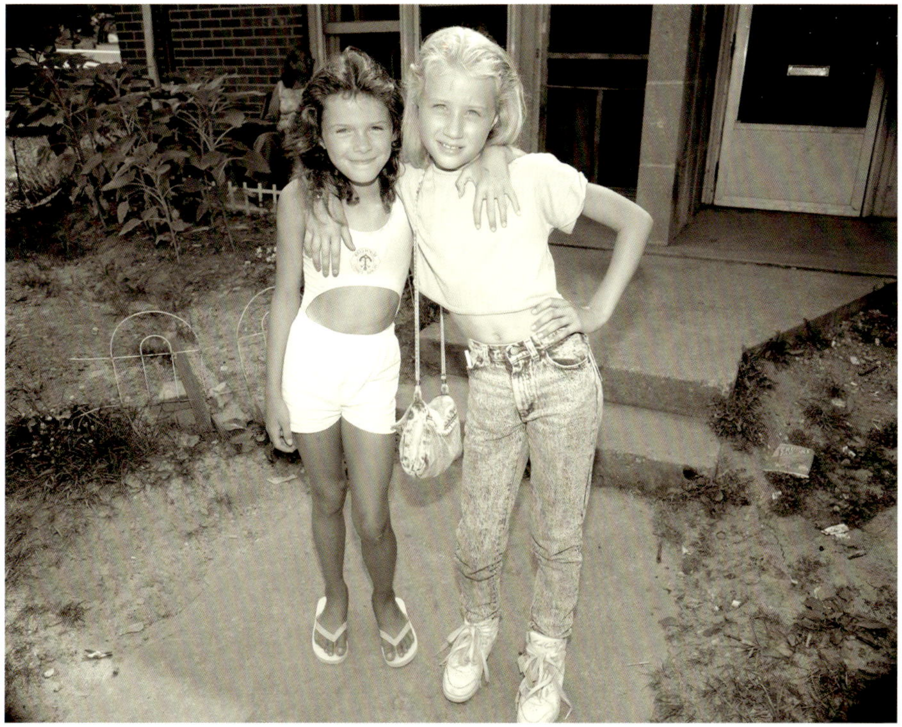

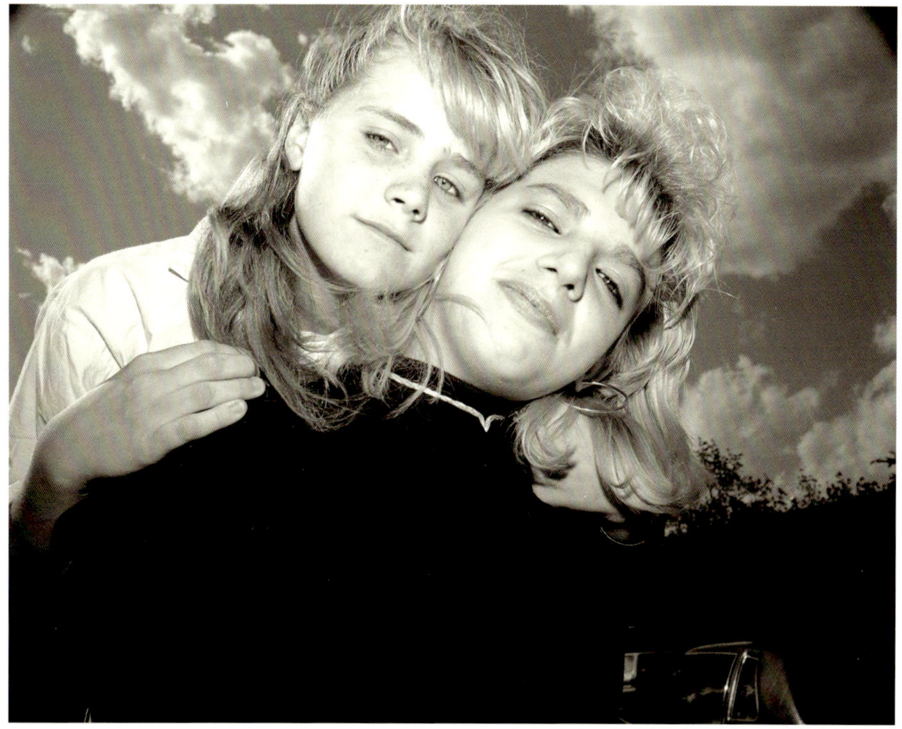

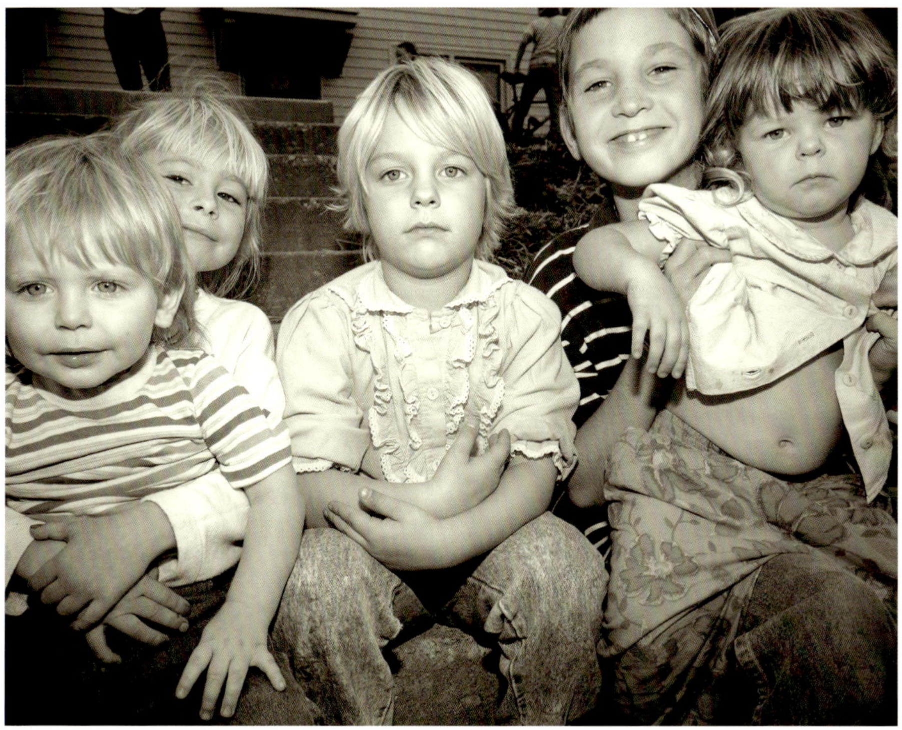

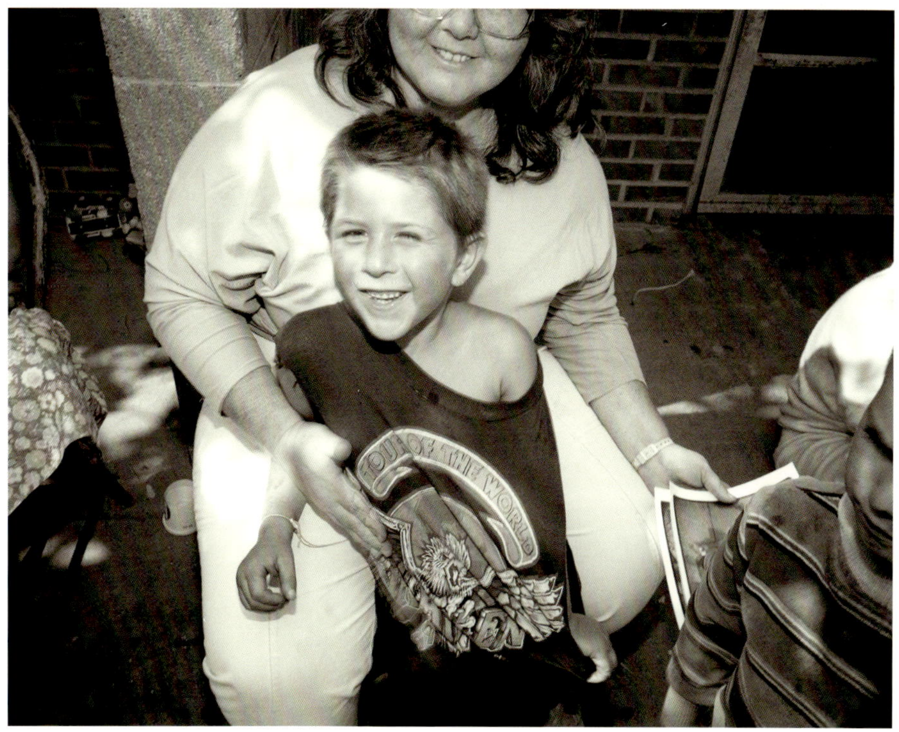

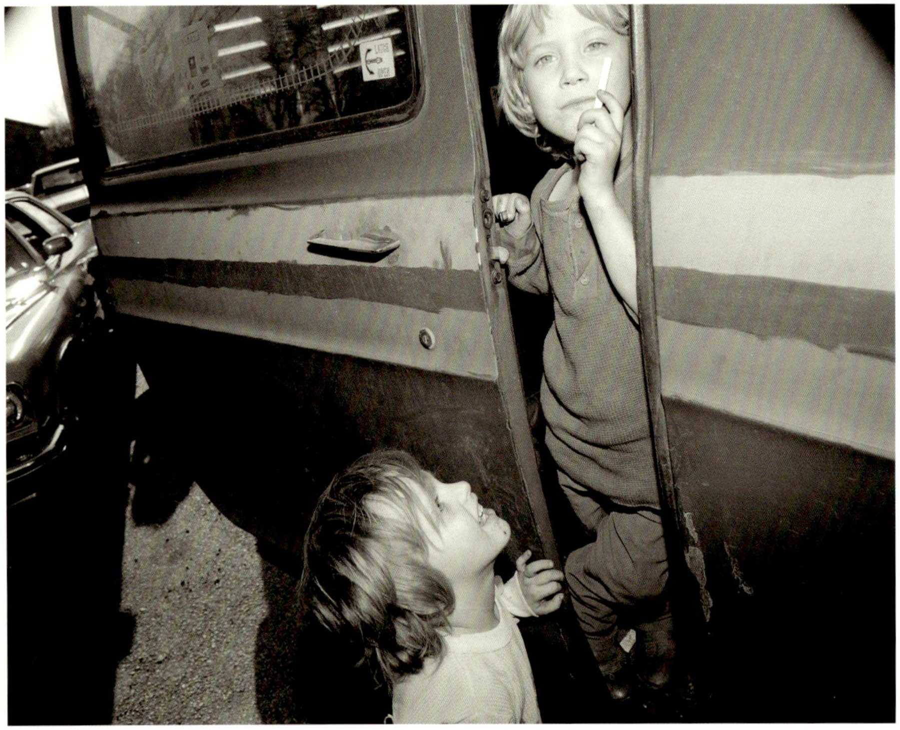
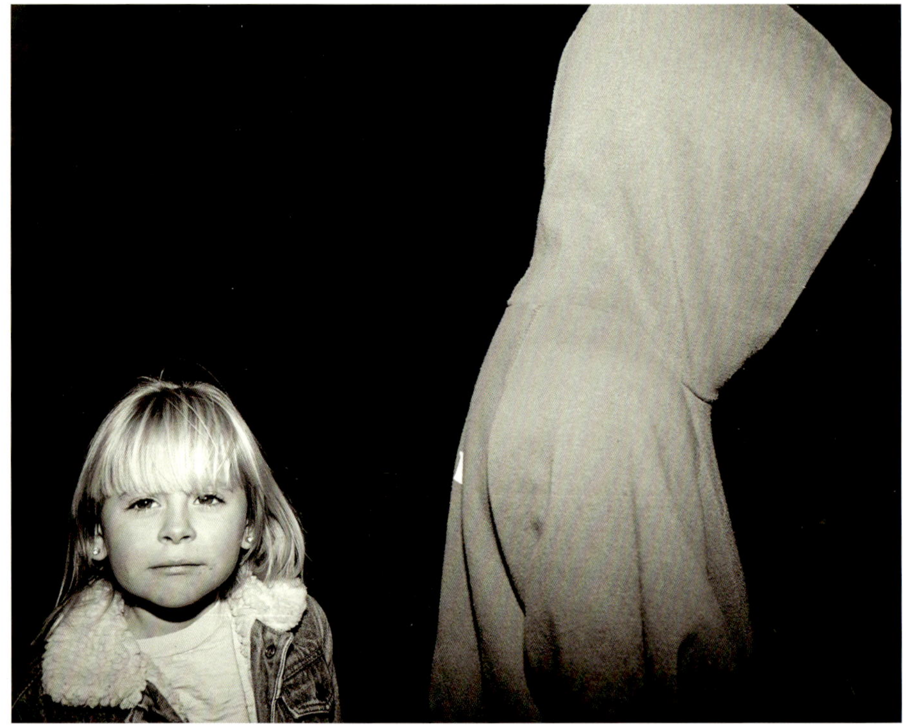
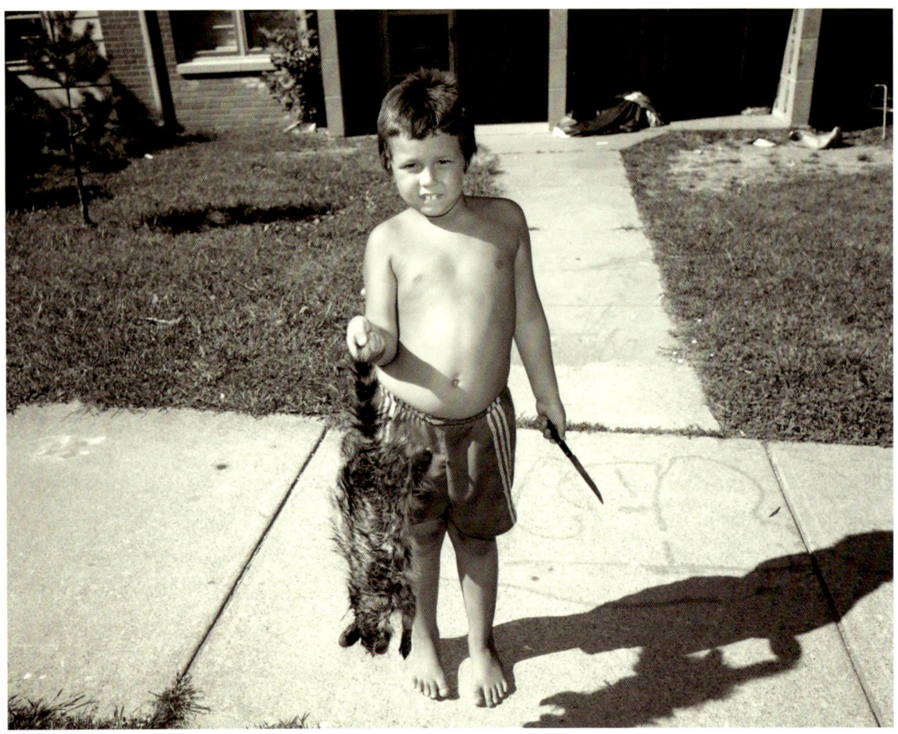
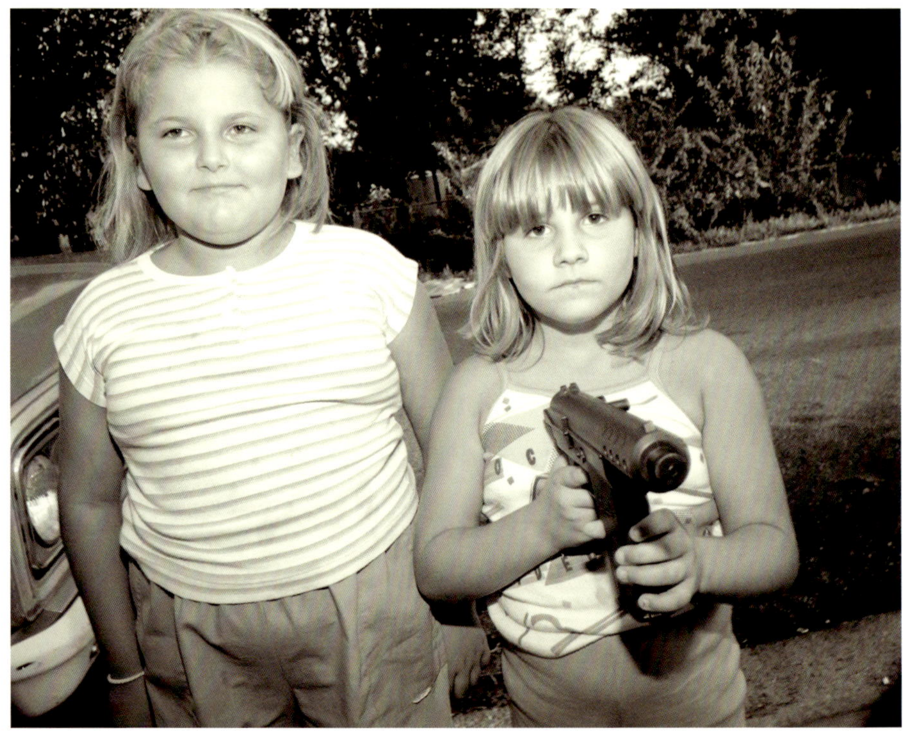

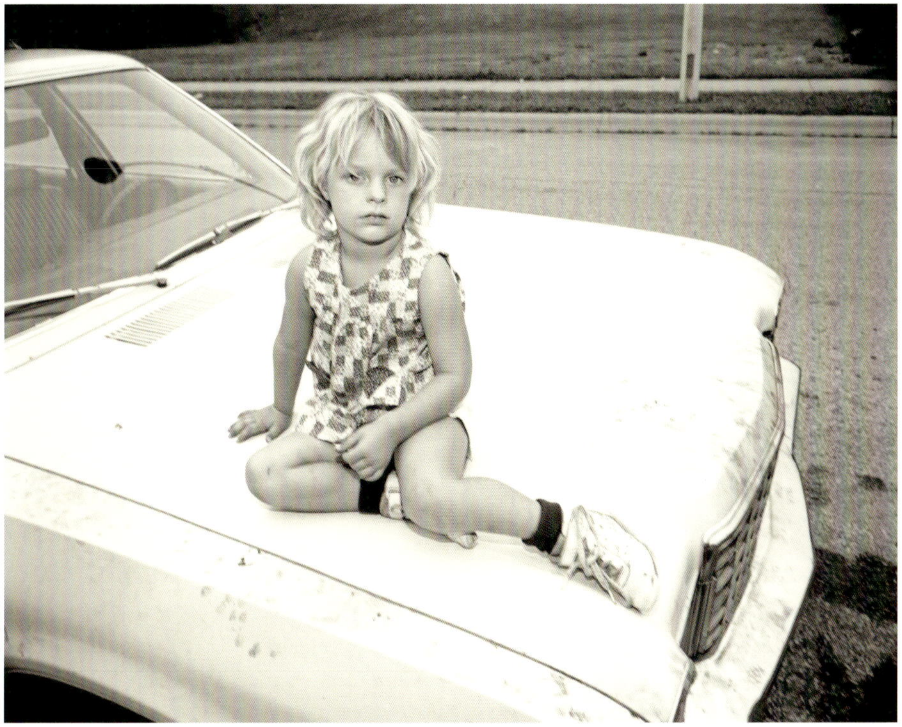

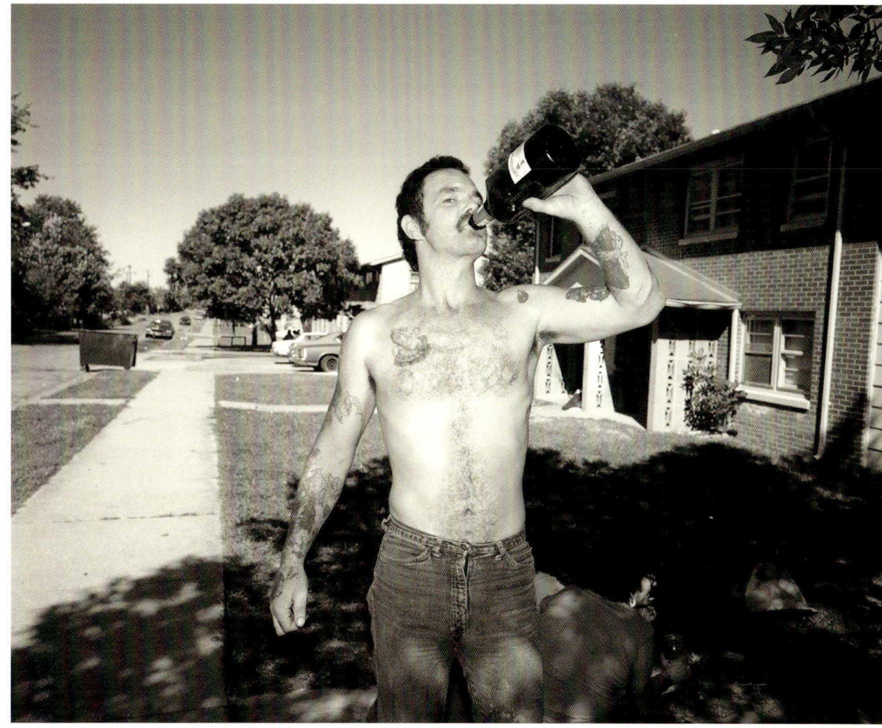

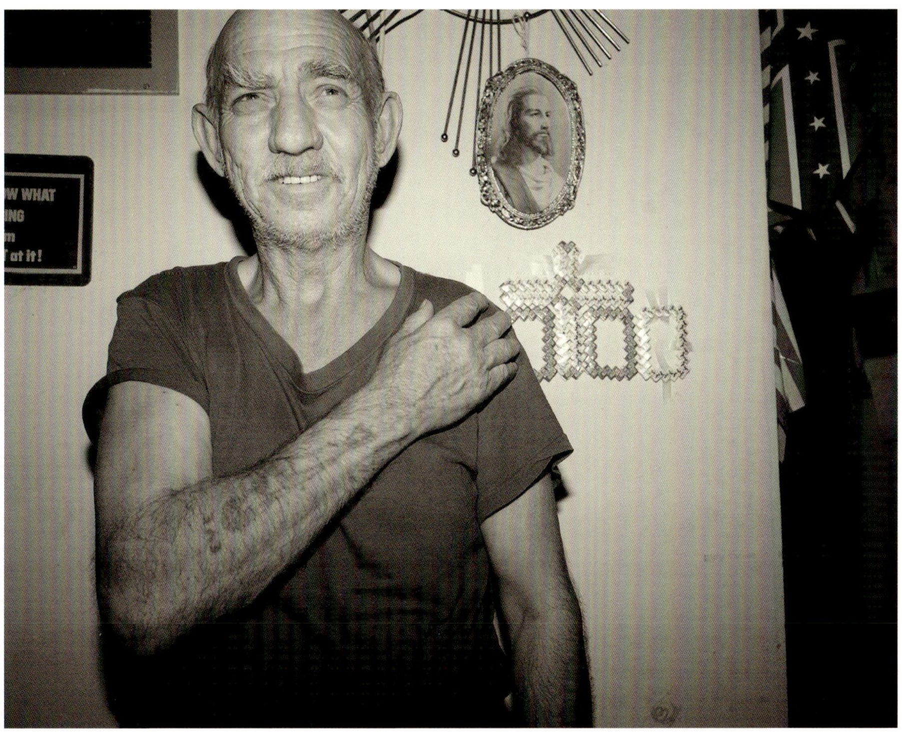

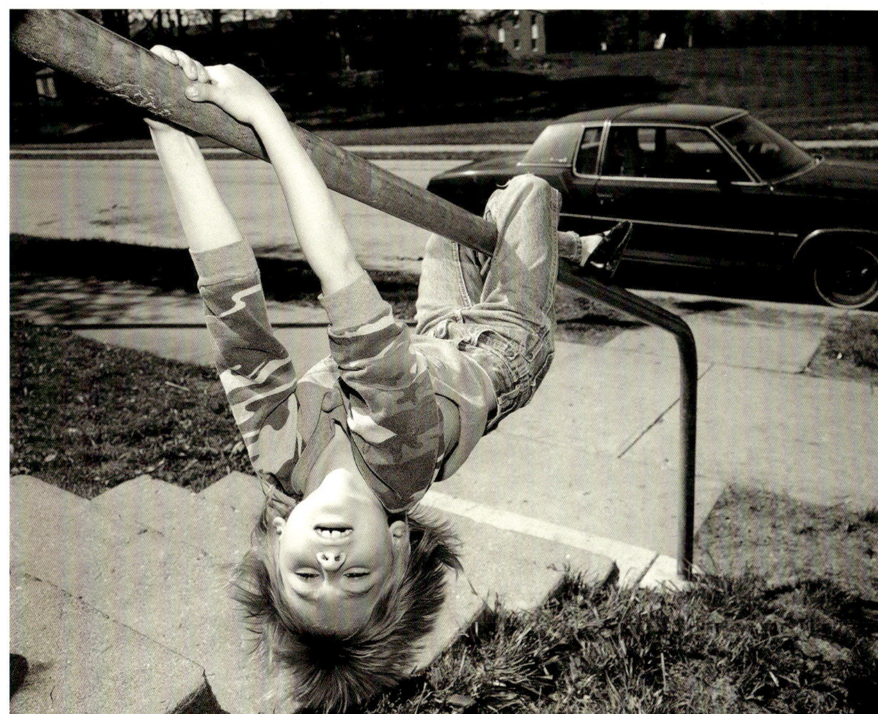

THEN &

NOW

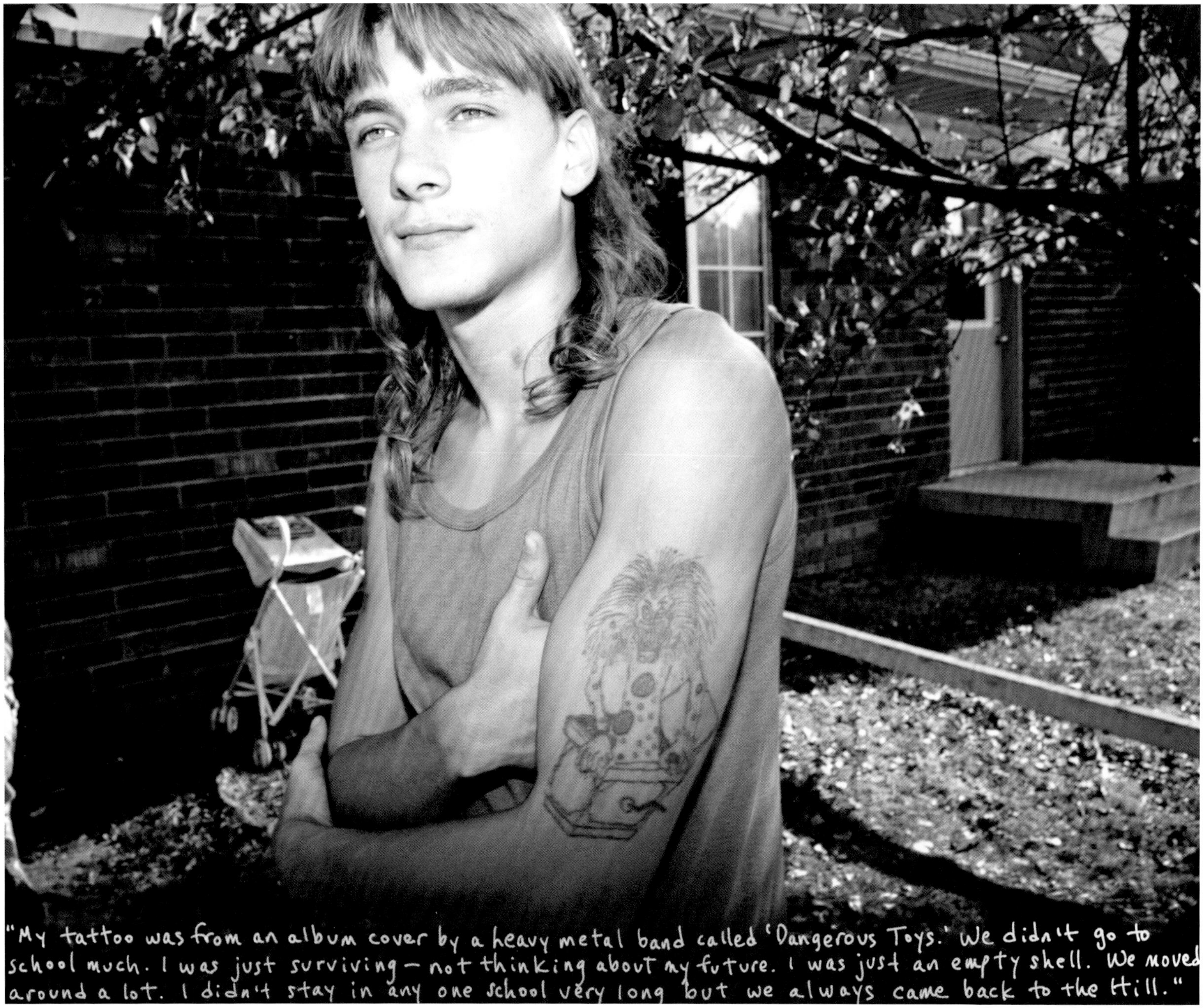

Jeff, Pigeon Hill, 1989

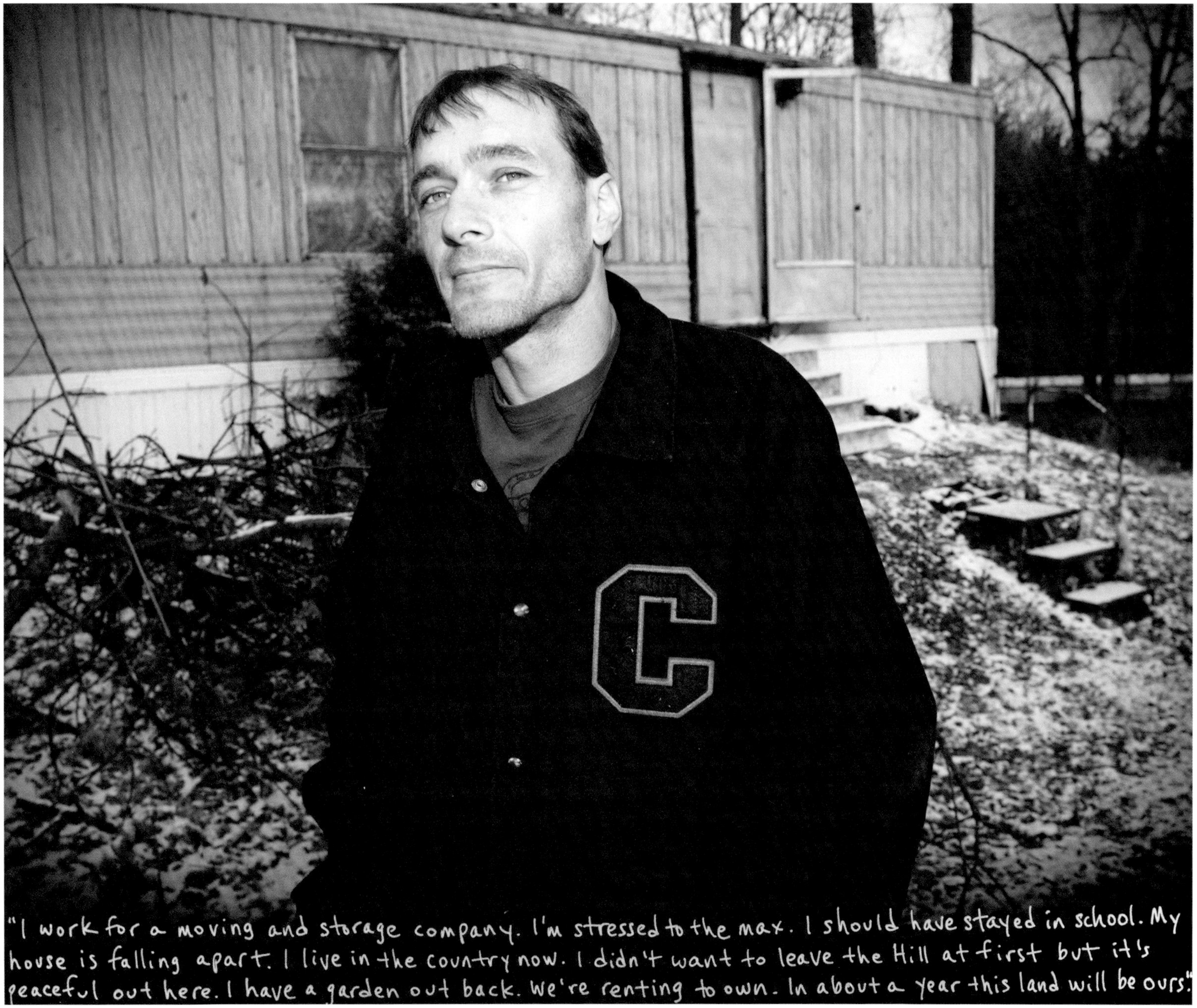

Jeff, Lawrence Hollow, 2012

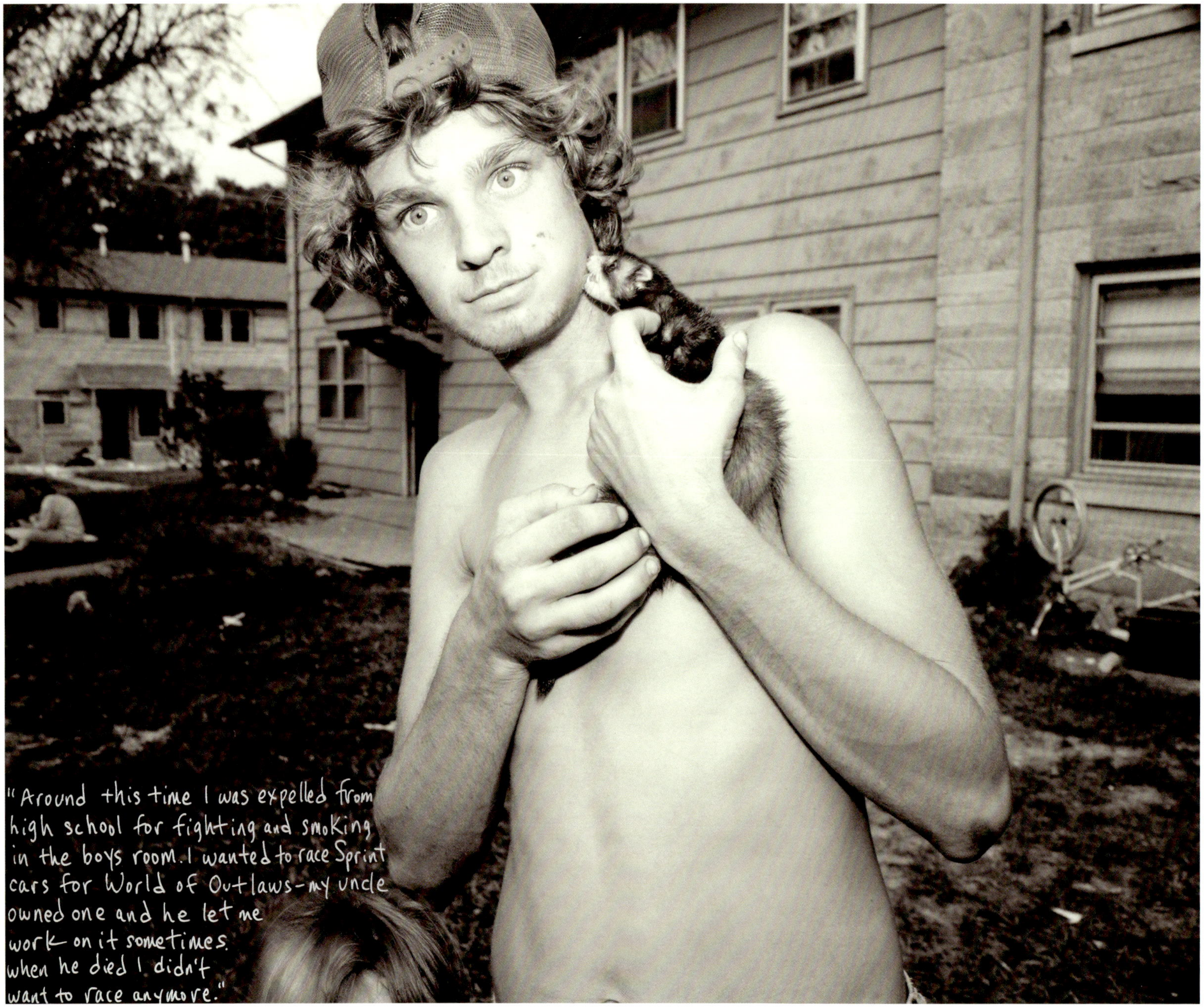

Timmy, Pigeon Hill, 1991

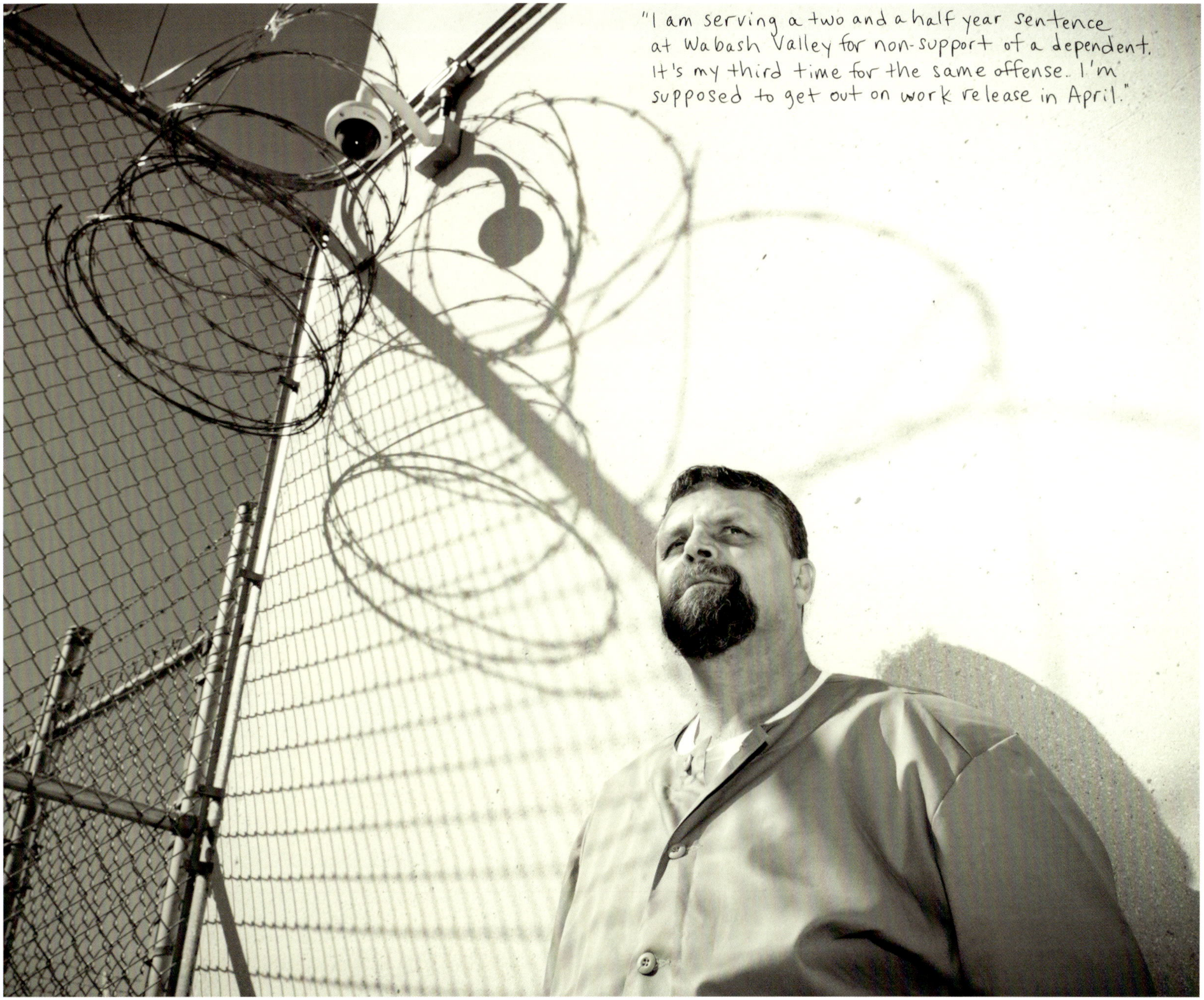

Timothy, Wabash Valley Correctional Facility, 2012

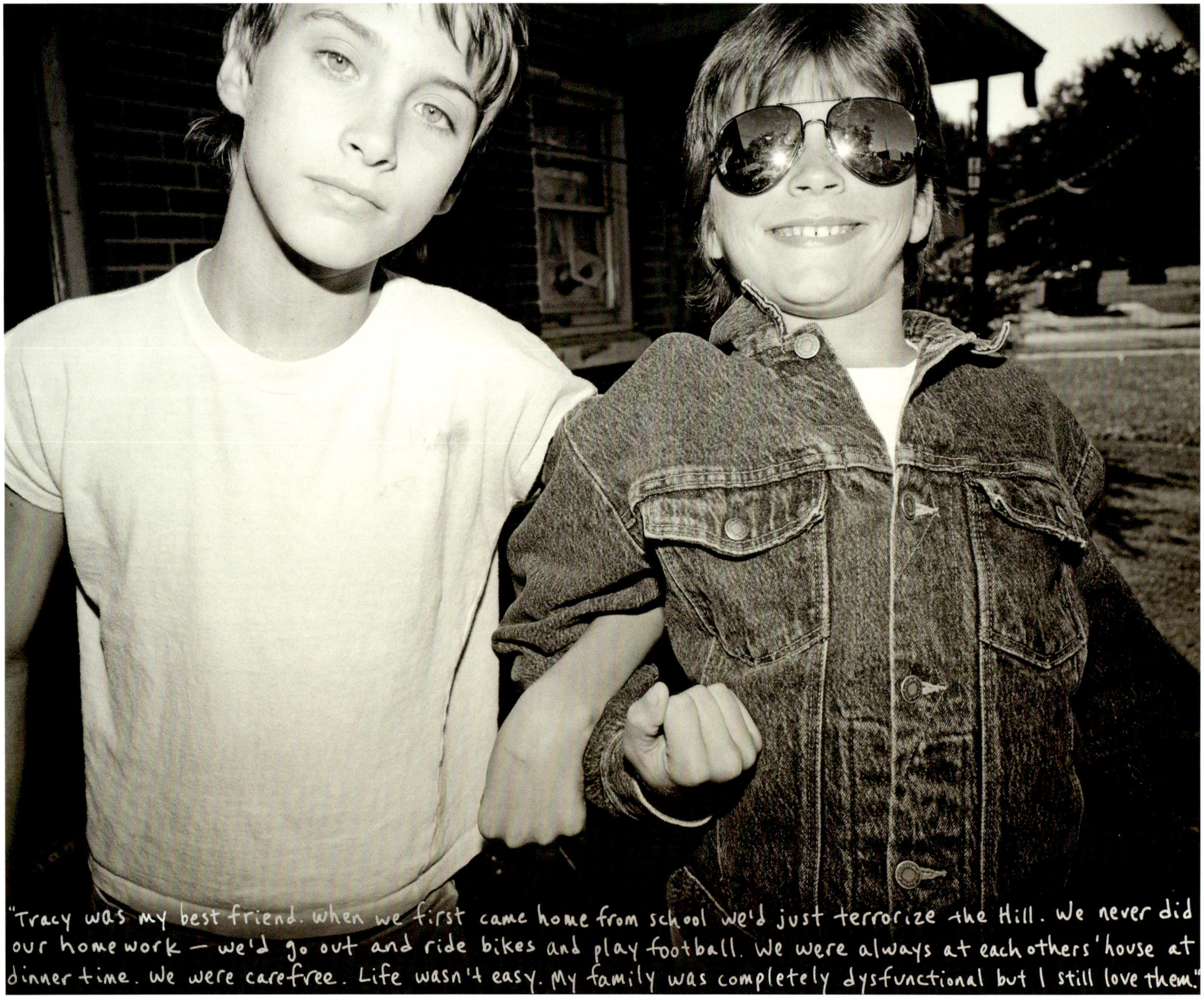

Robert with Tracy, Pigeon Hill, 1989

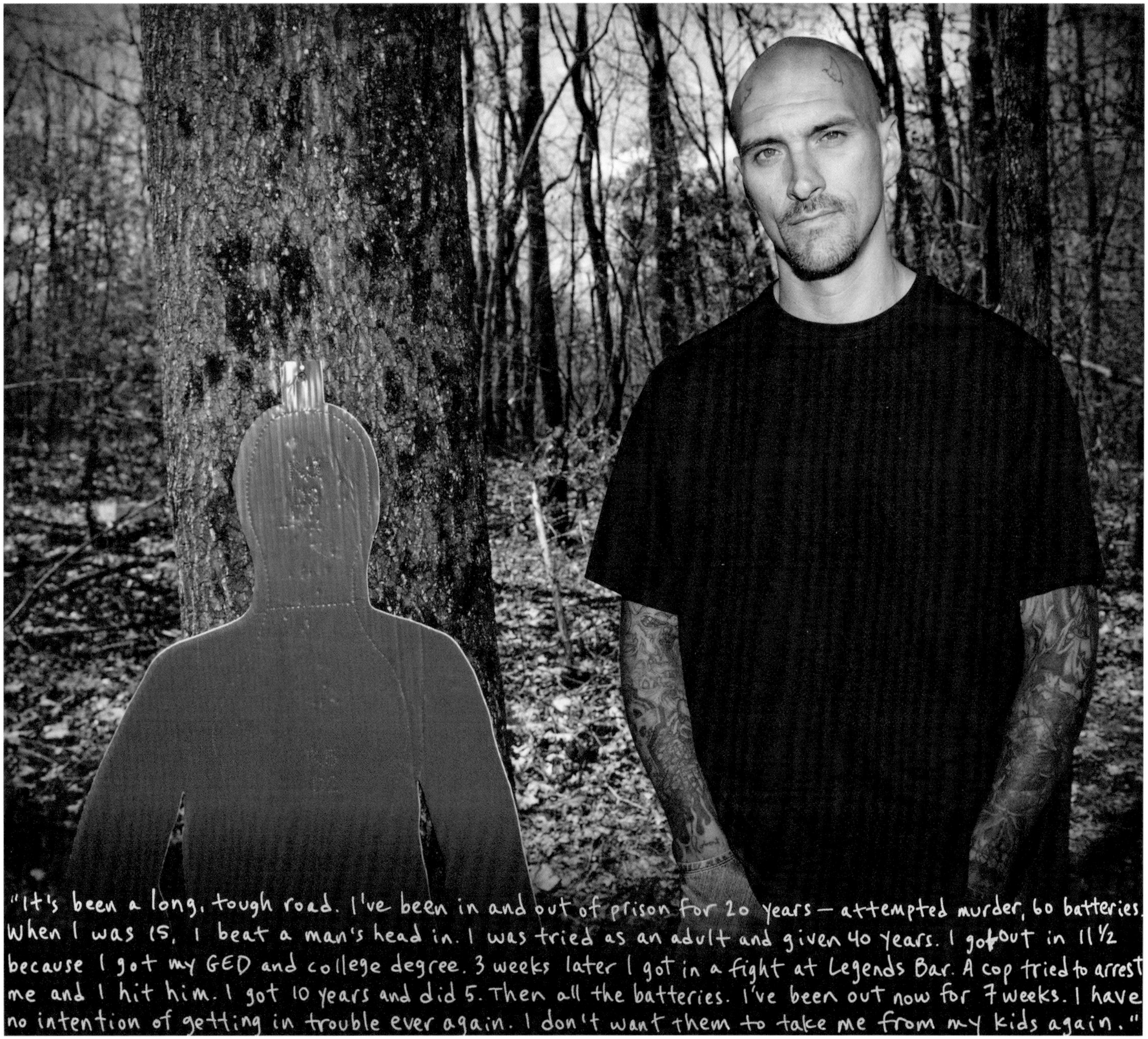

Robert, North Oolitic Drive, Pigeon Hill, 2013

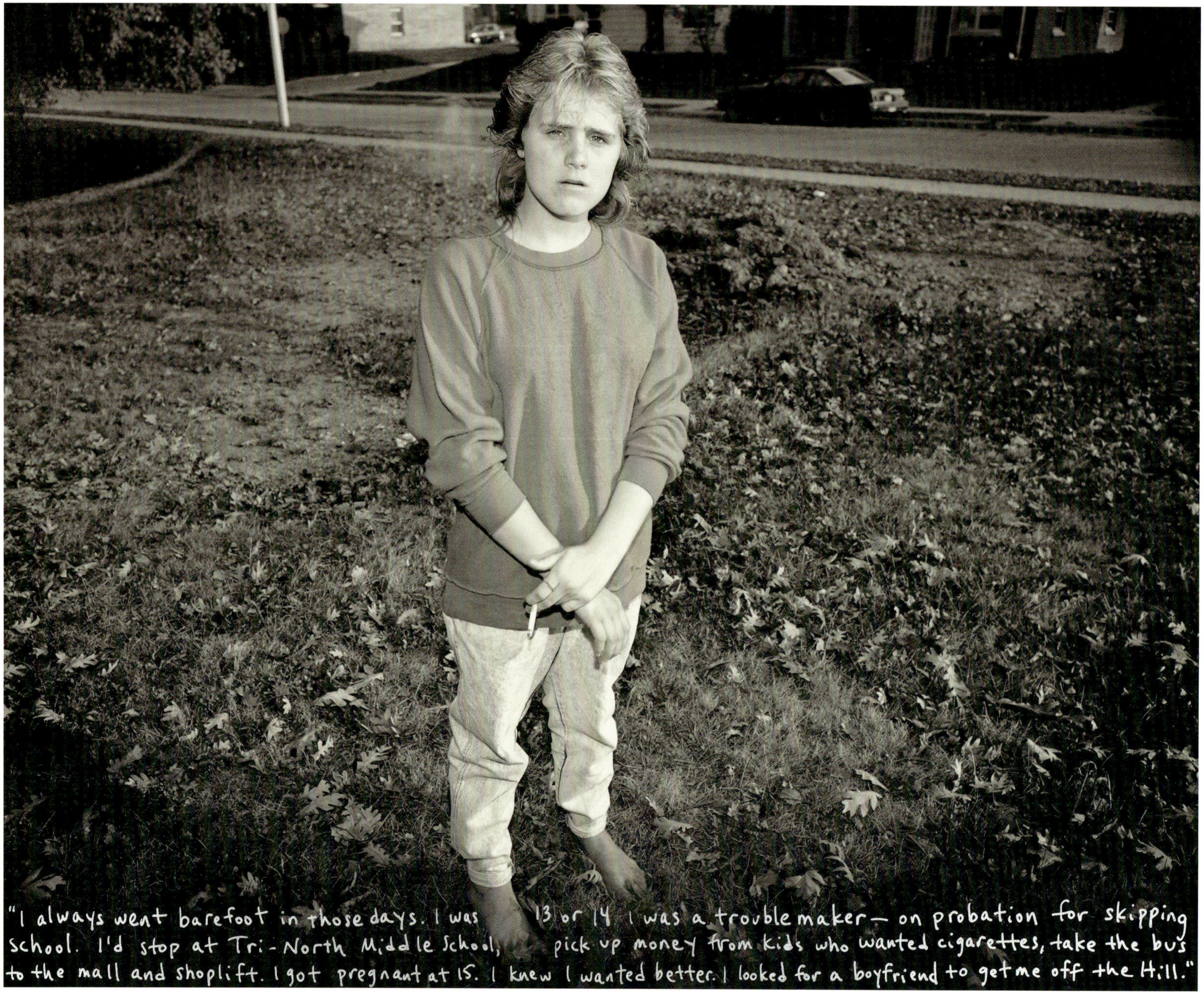

Angie with Cigarette, Pigeon Hill, 1990

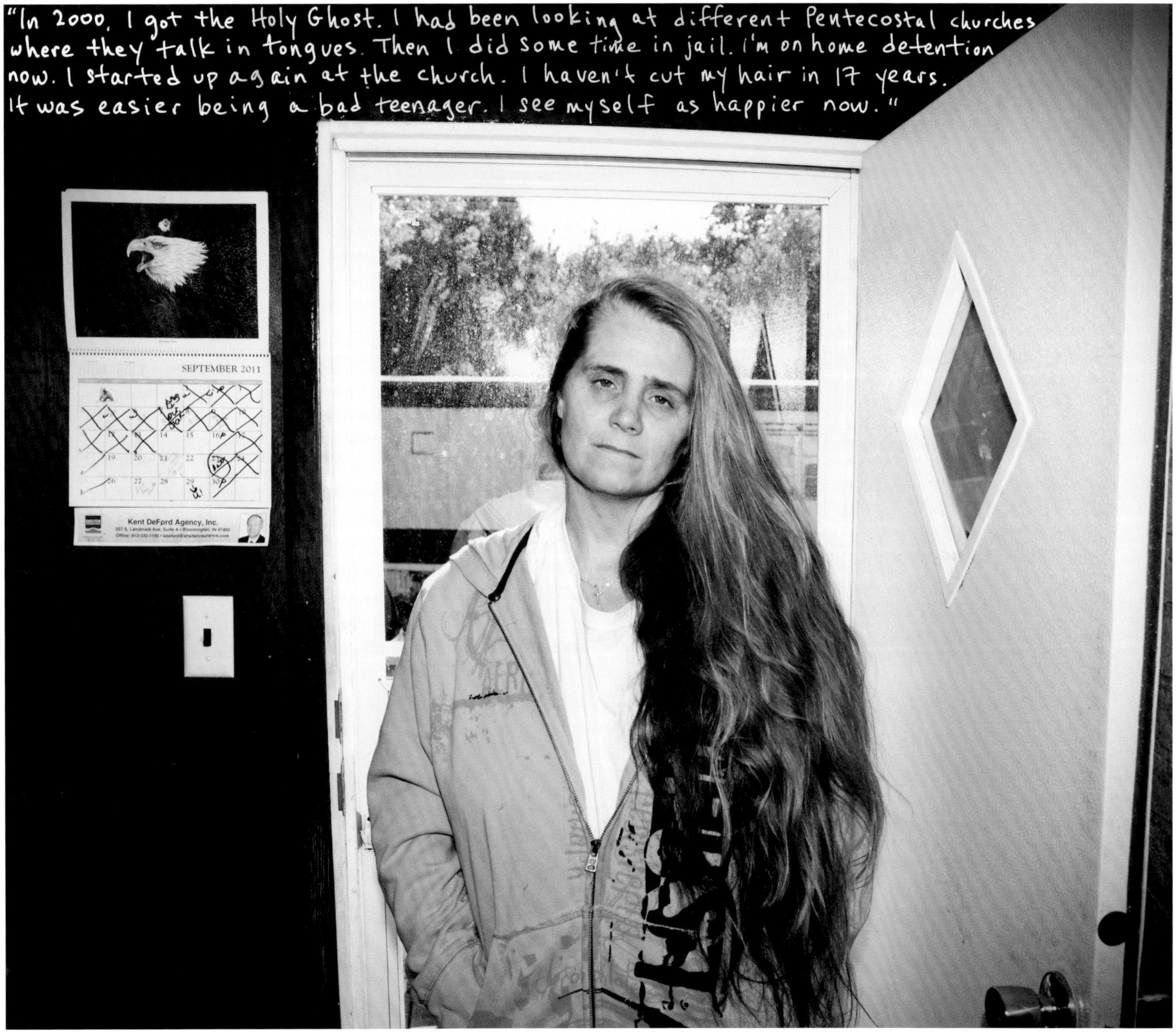

Angie, Lenzy Hayes Trailer Park, Ellettsville, 2011

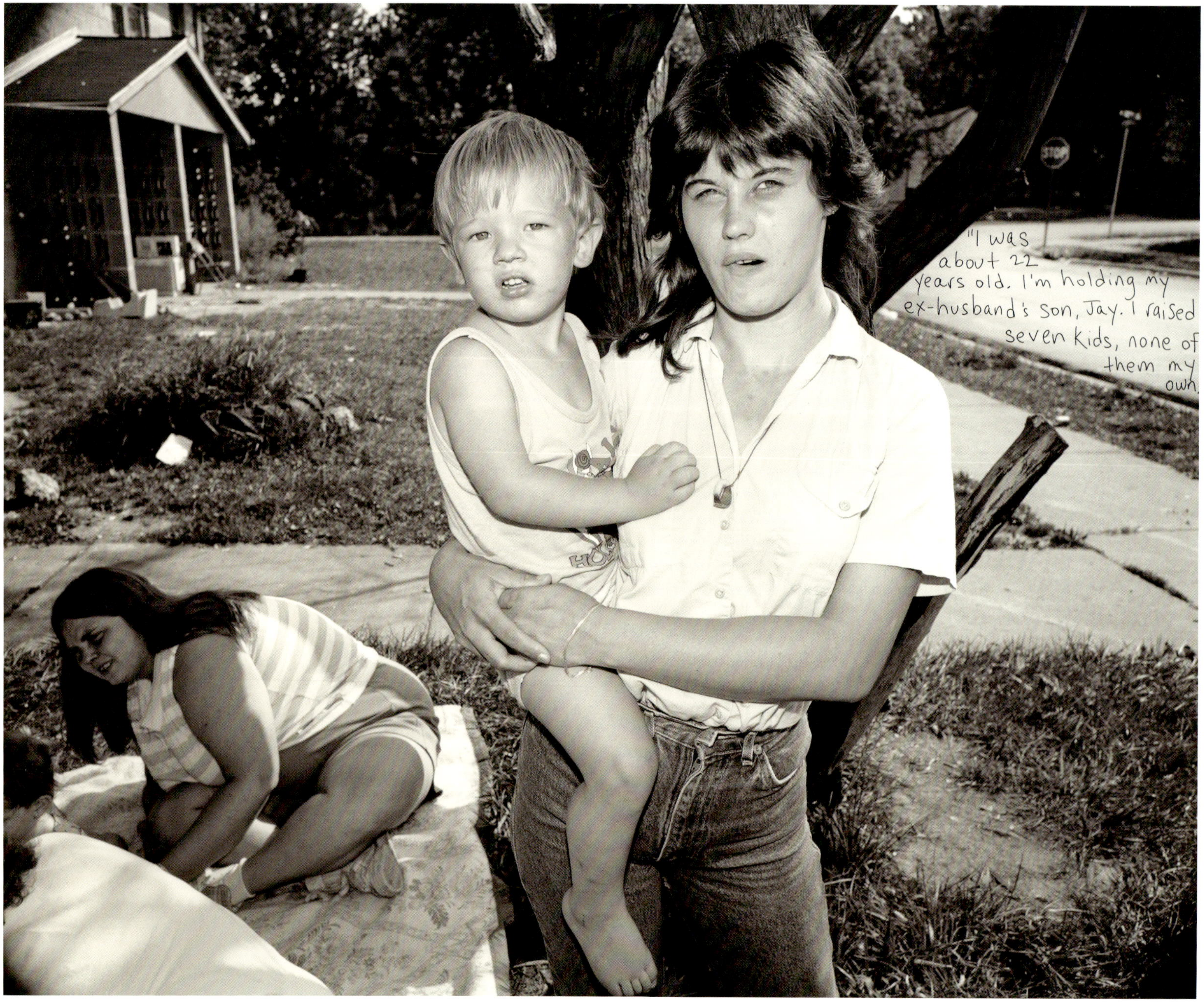

Tina and Jay, 1988

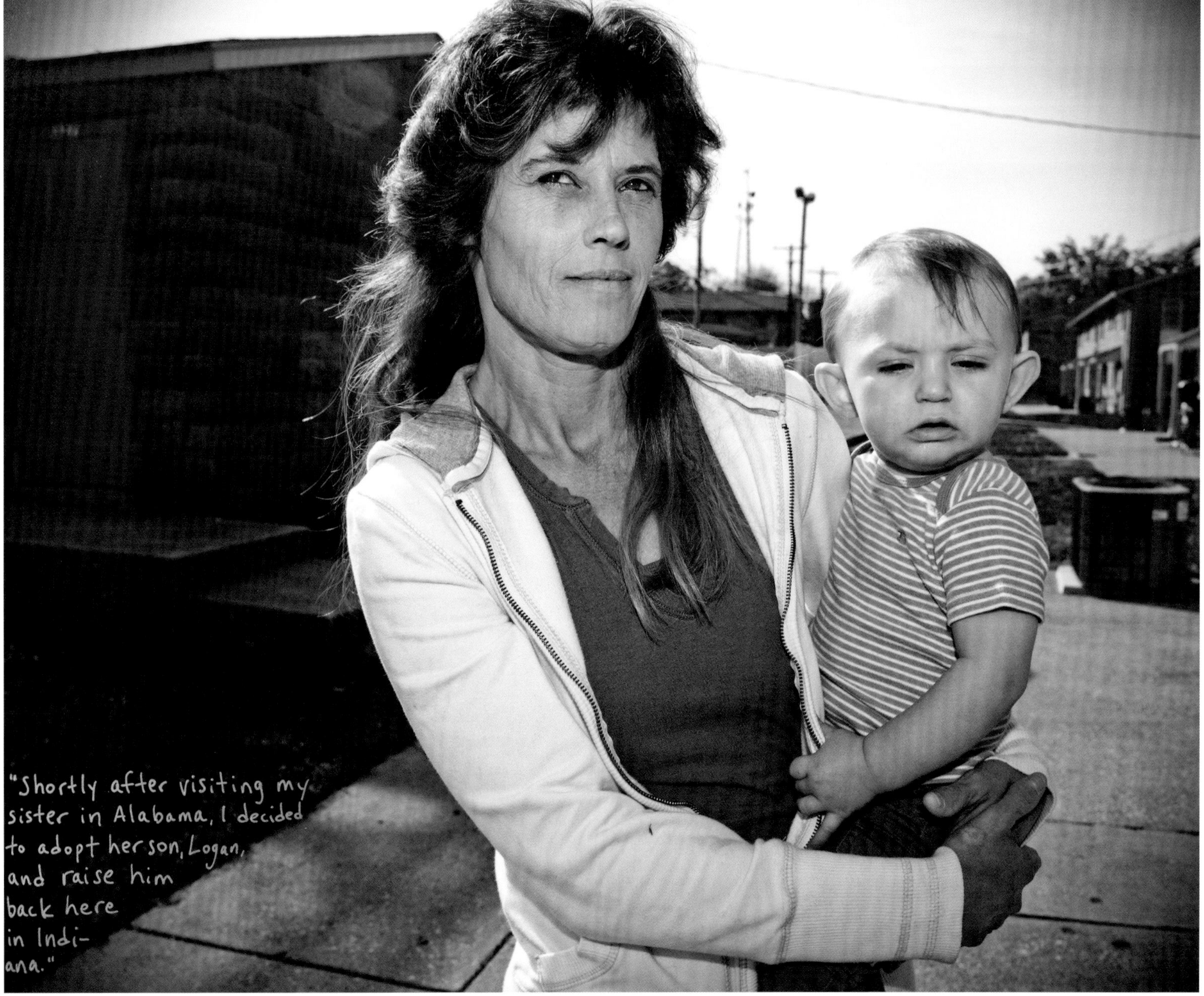

Tina and Logan, Pigeon Hill, 2012

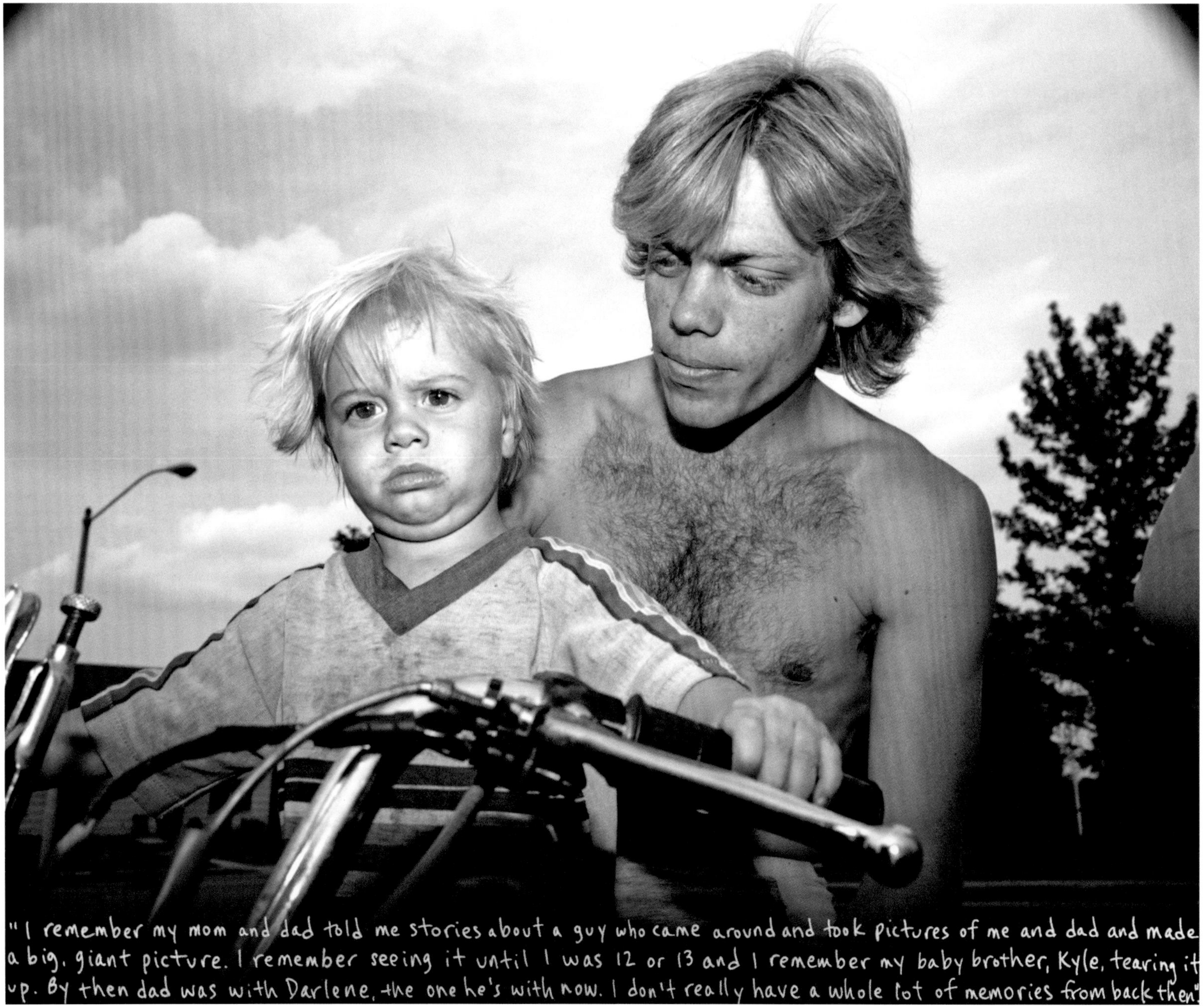

Marvin Jr. and Marvin Sr., Pigeon Hill, 1991

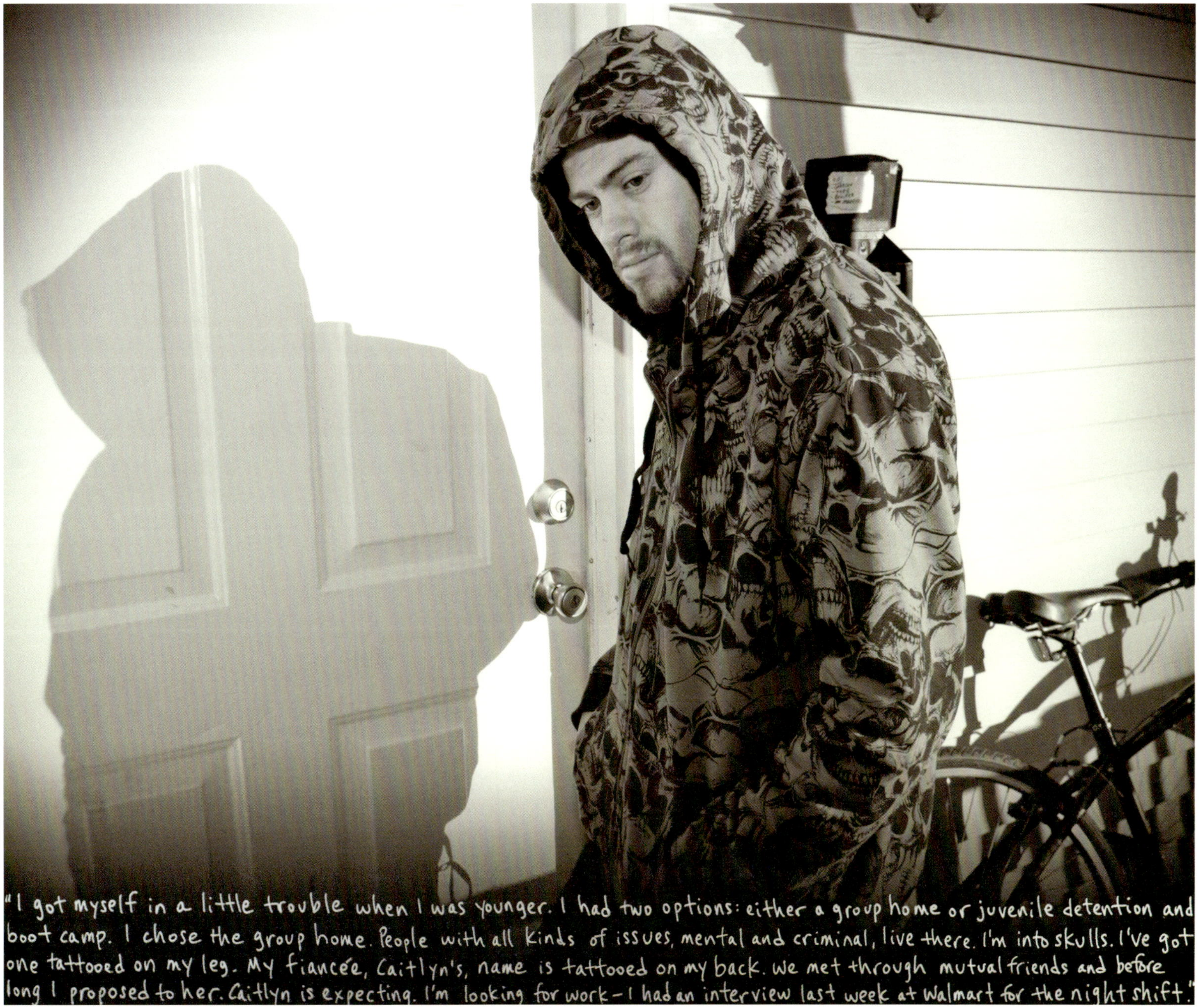

Marvin Jr. at Group Home, Bloomington, 2012

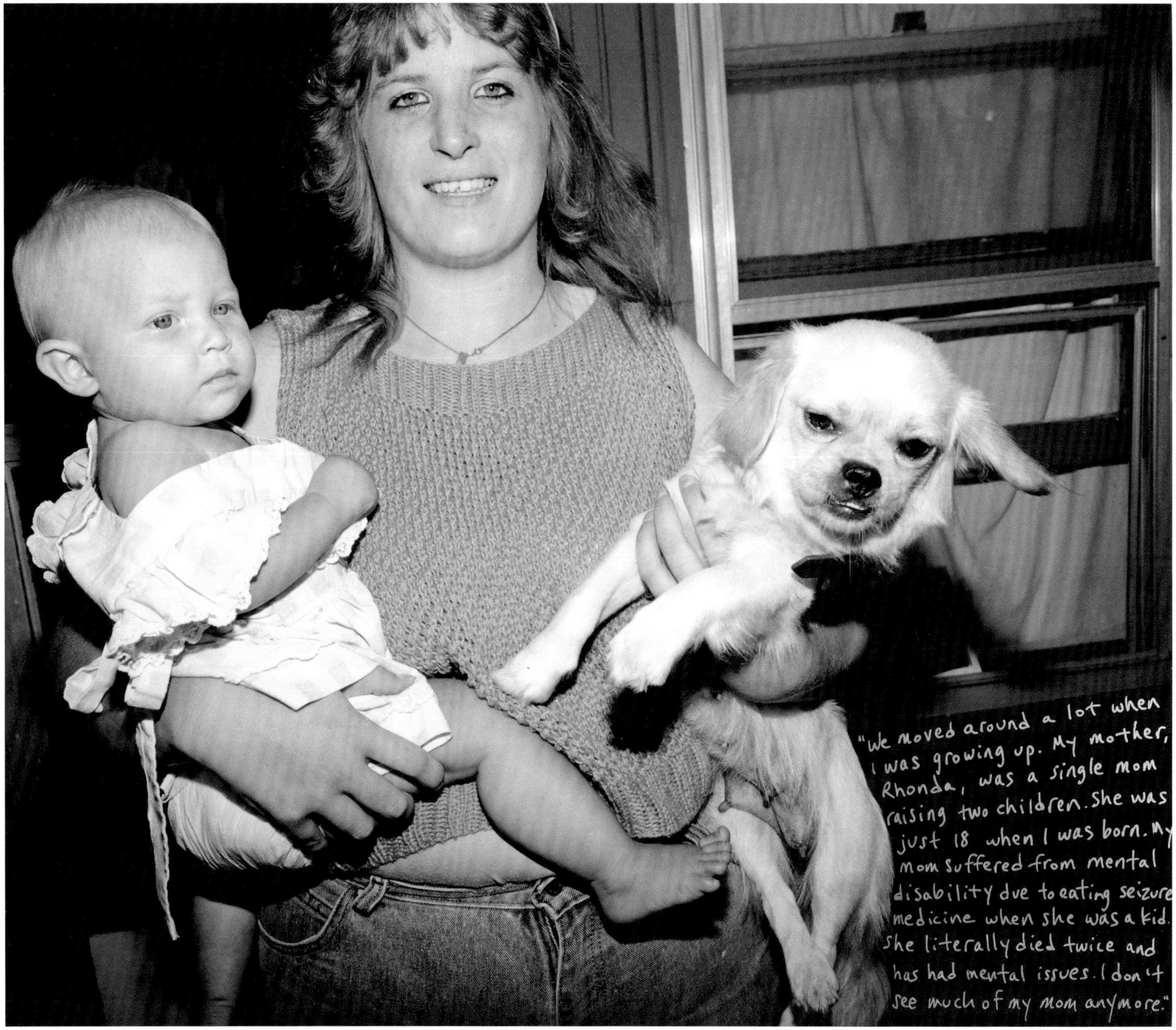

Justin and Rhonda with Stormy, Pigeon Hill, 1988

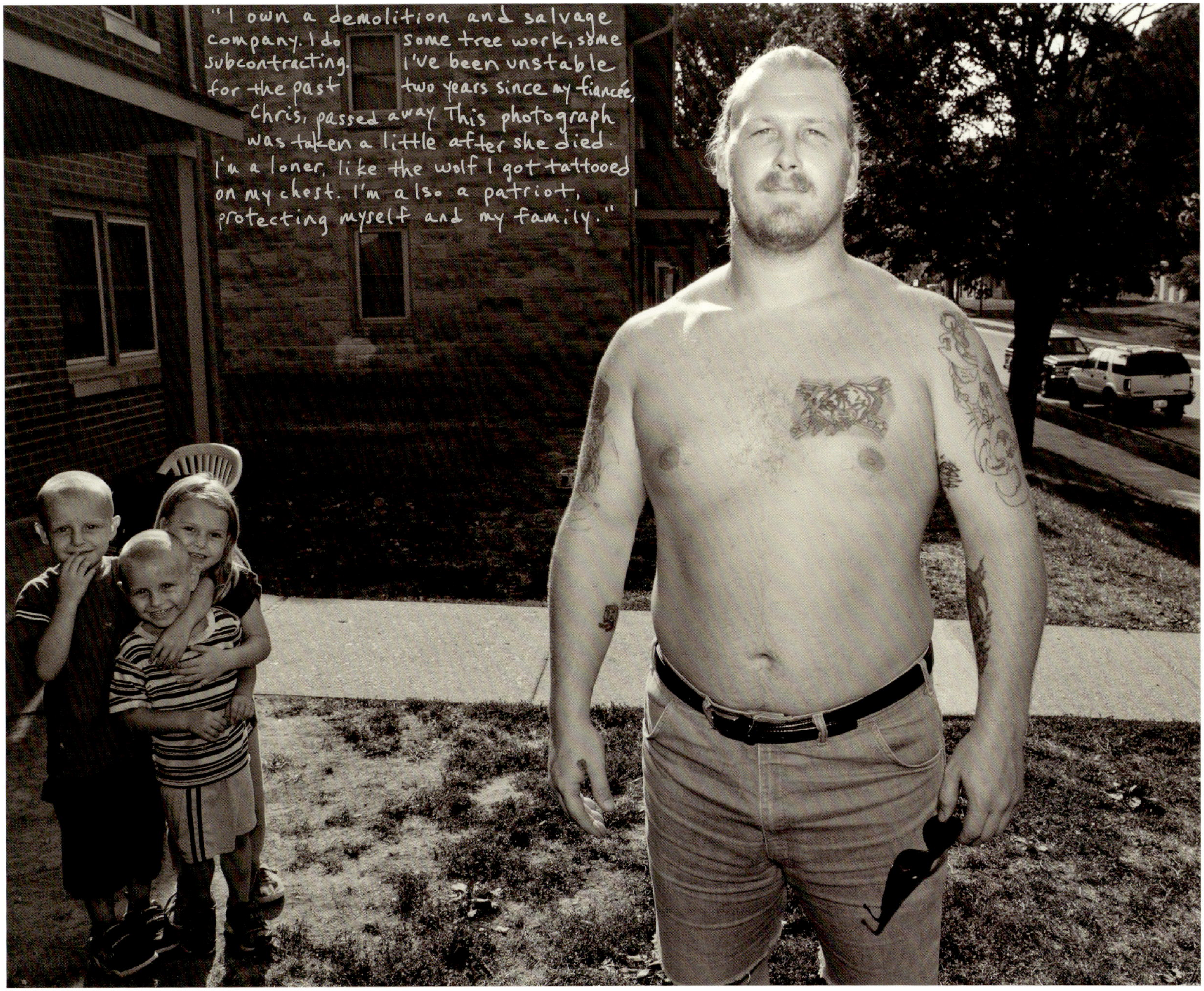

Justin after his Fiancée Died, Pigeon Hill, 2011

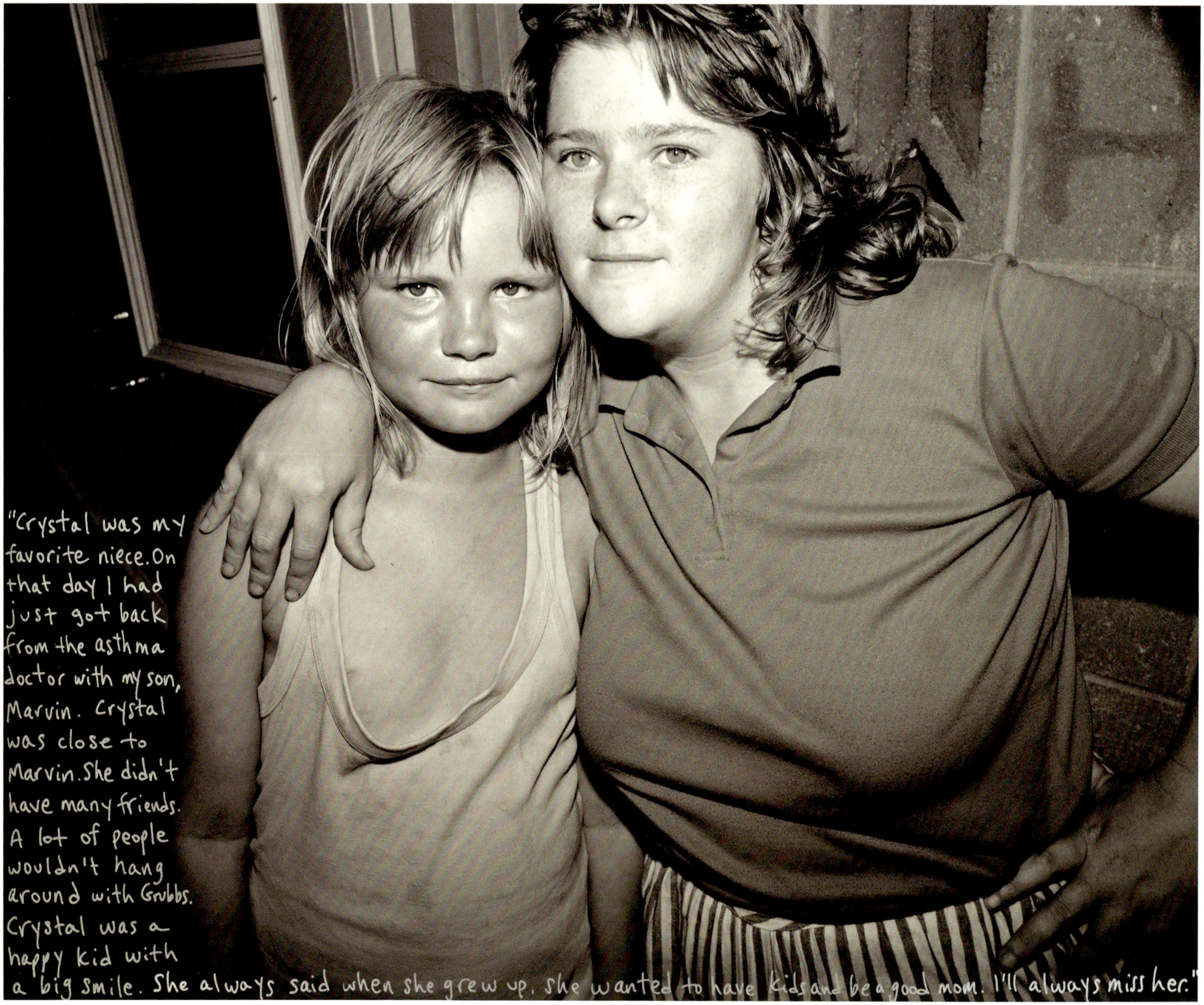

Crystal and her Aunt Judy, Pigeon Hill, 1991

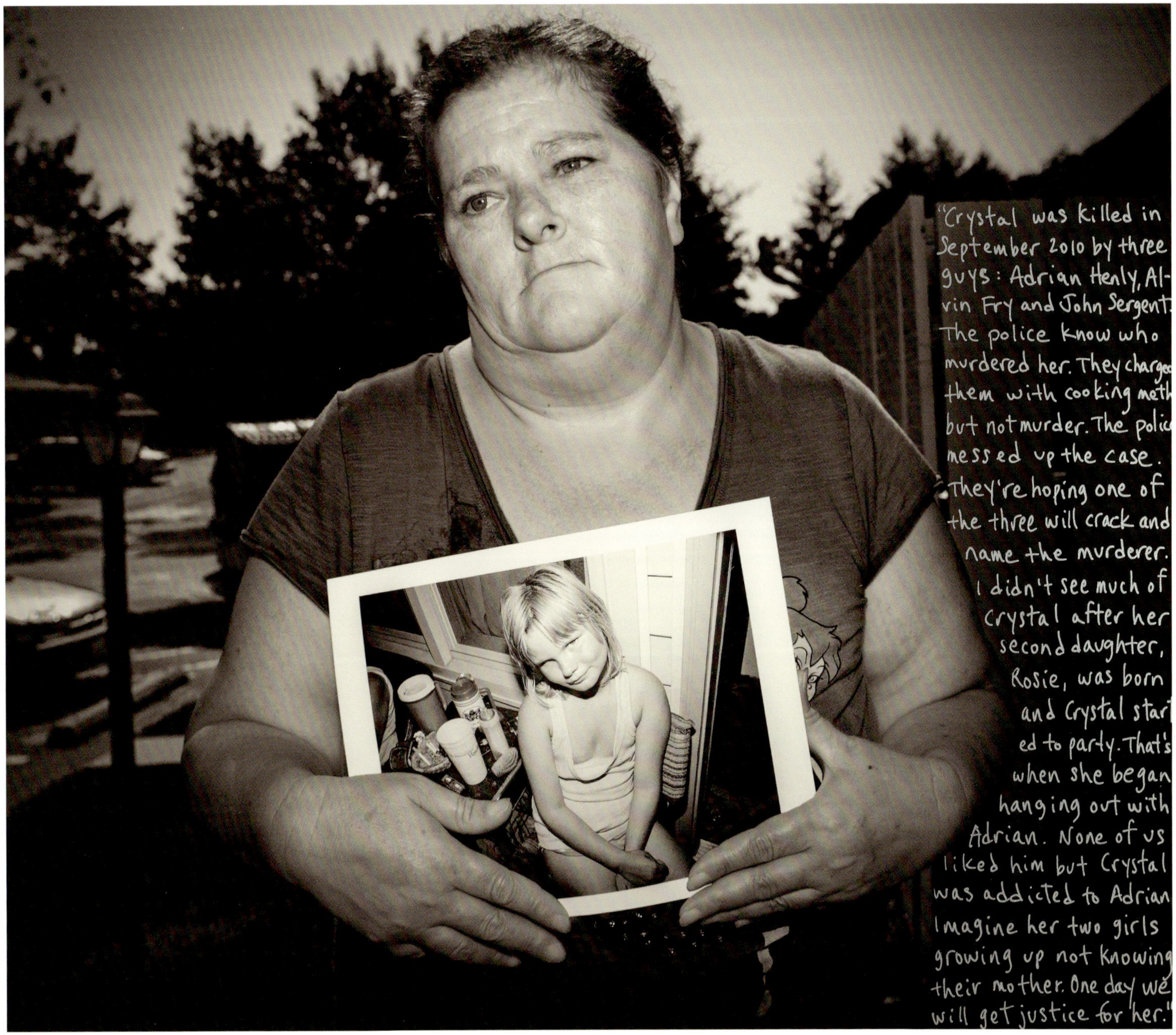

Judy after Crystal's Murder, Acadia Court, 2013

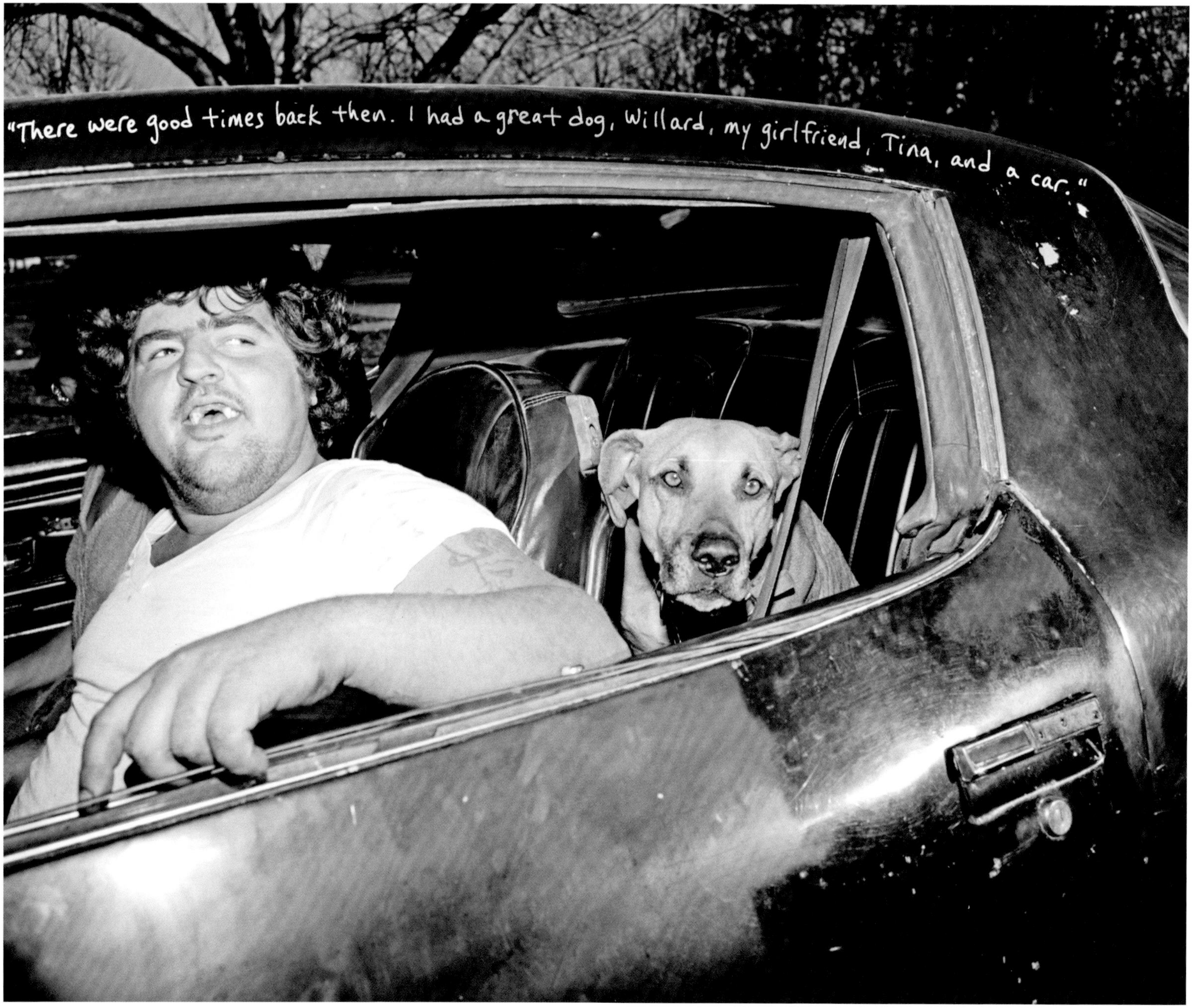

Danny, Pigeon Hill, 1988

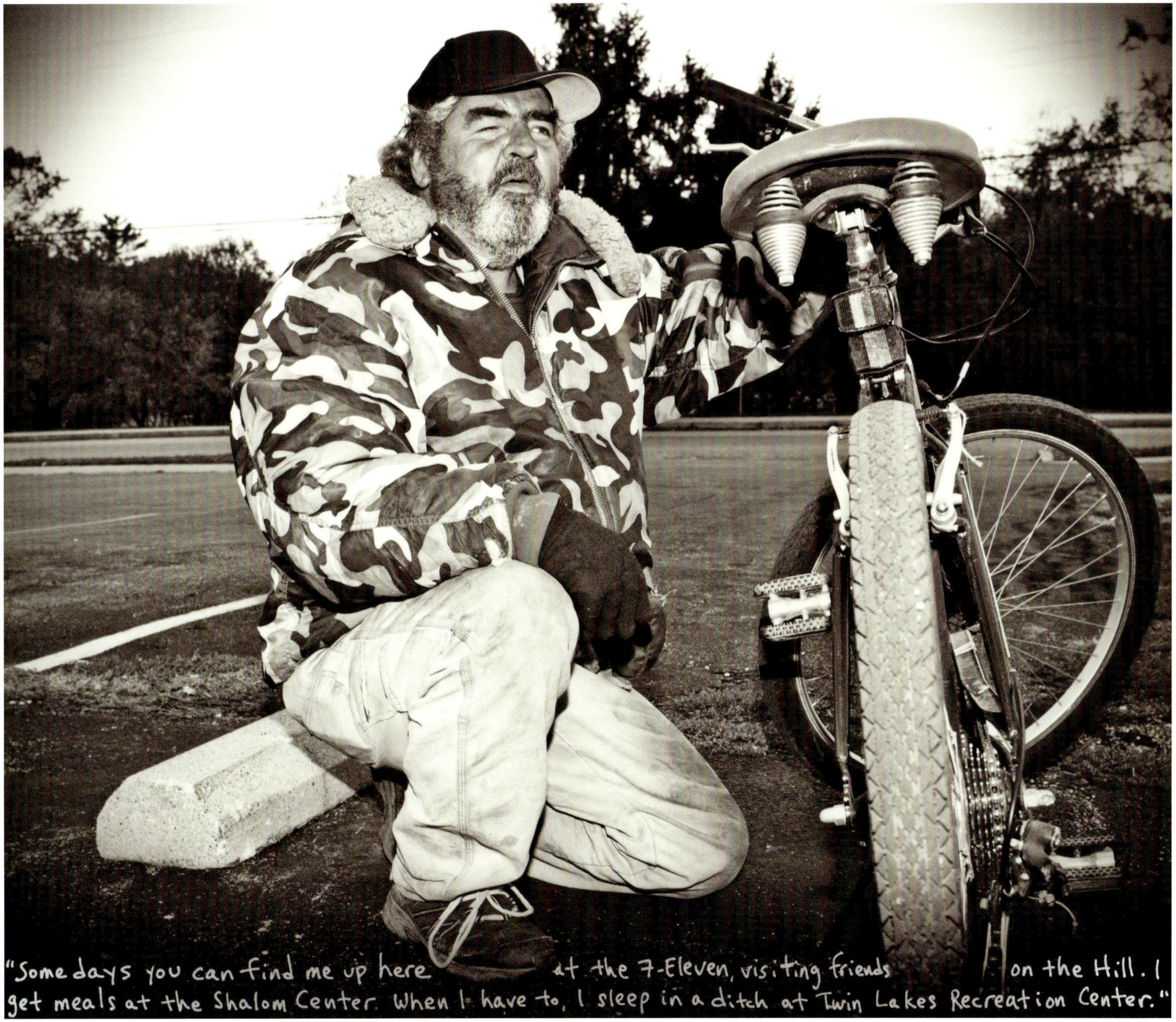

Danny, 7-Eleven, Pigeon Hill, 2012

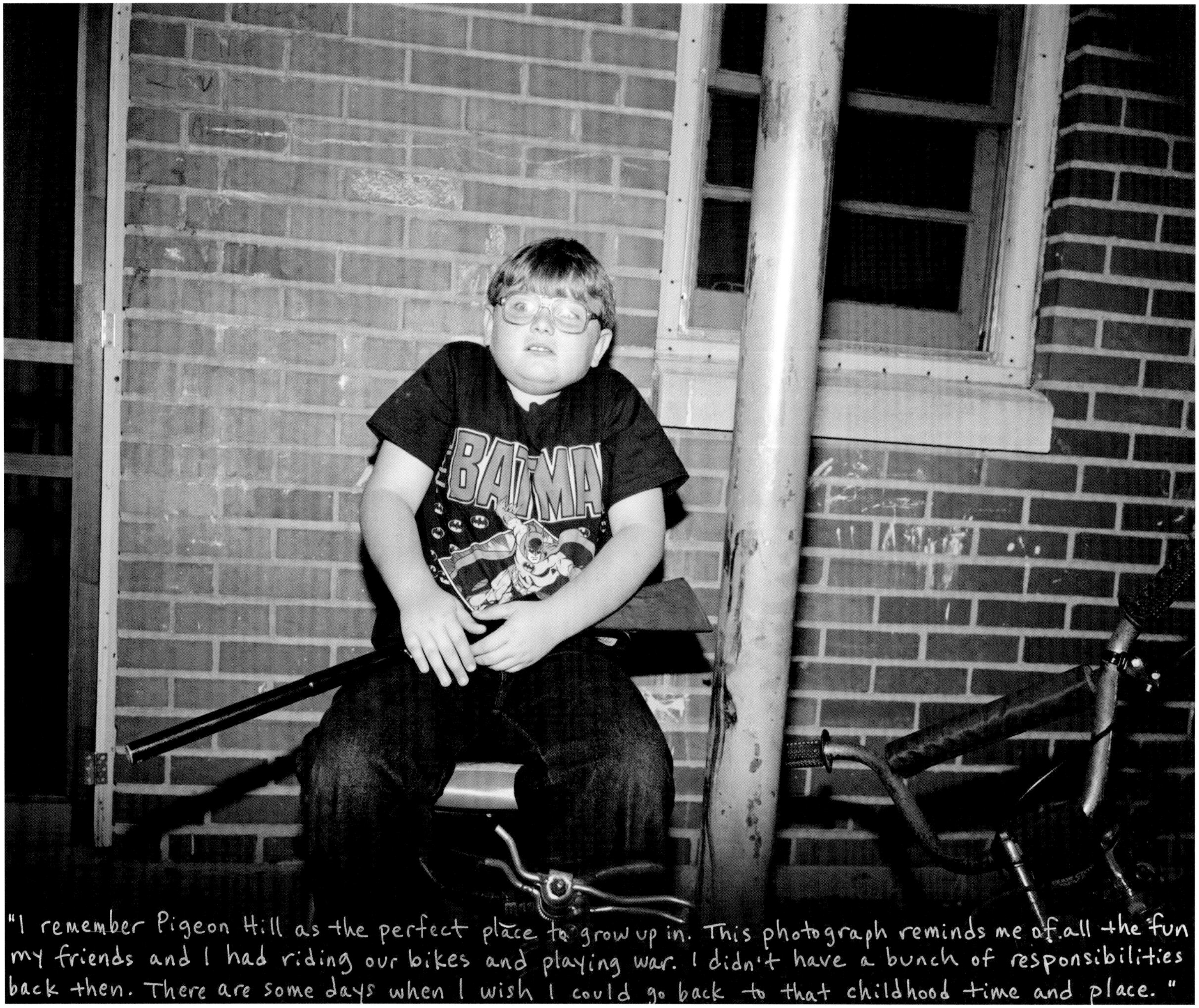

"Tyke", Pigeon Hill, 1989

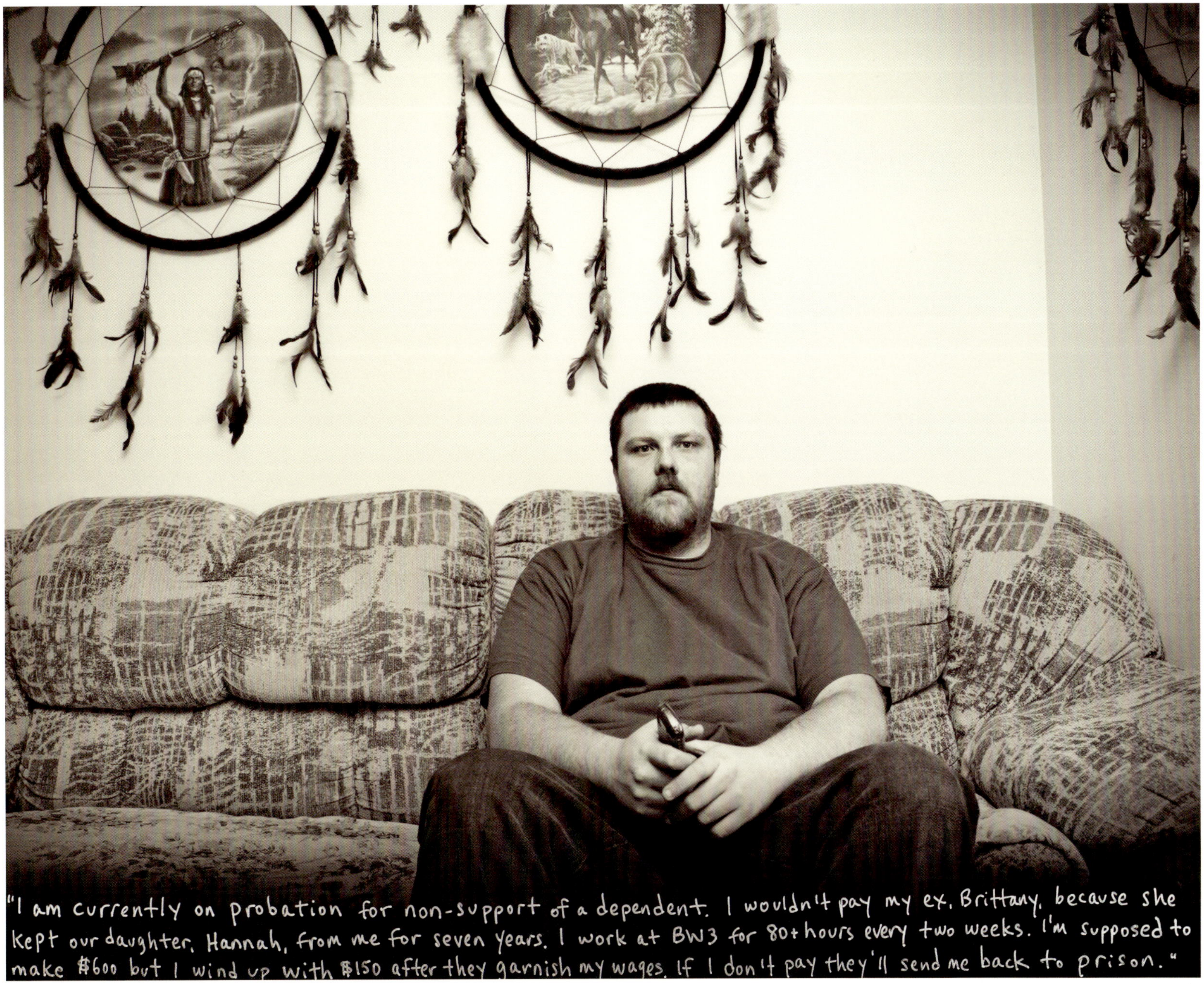

David, Arlington Park Apartments, 2011

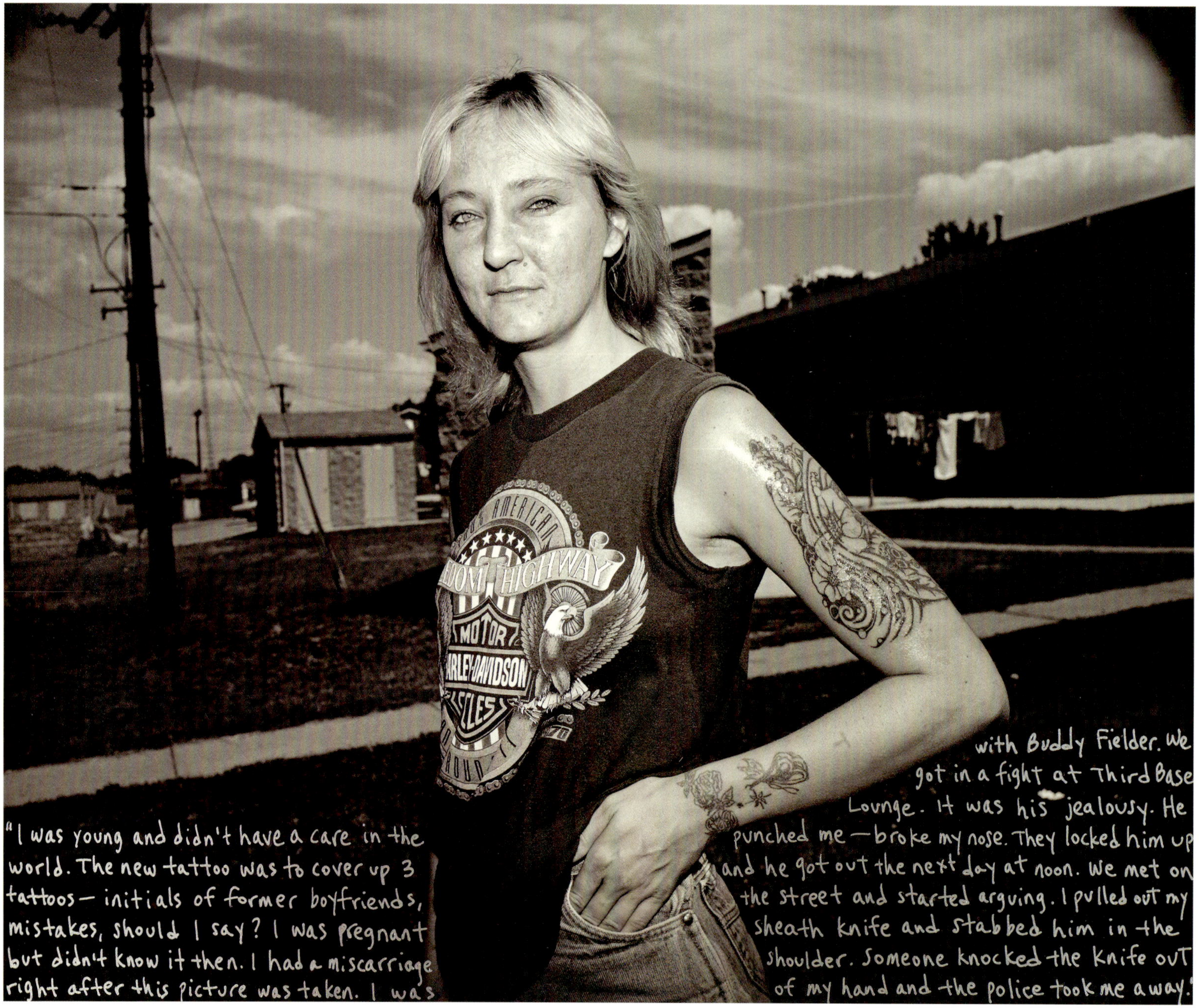

Tina with New Tattoo, Pigeon Hill, 1991

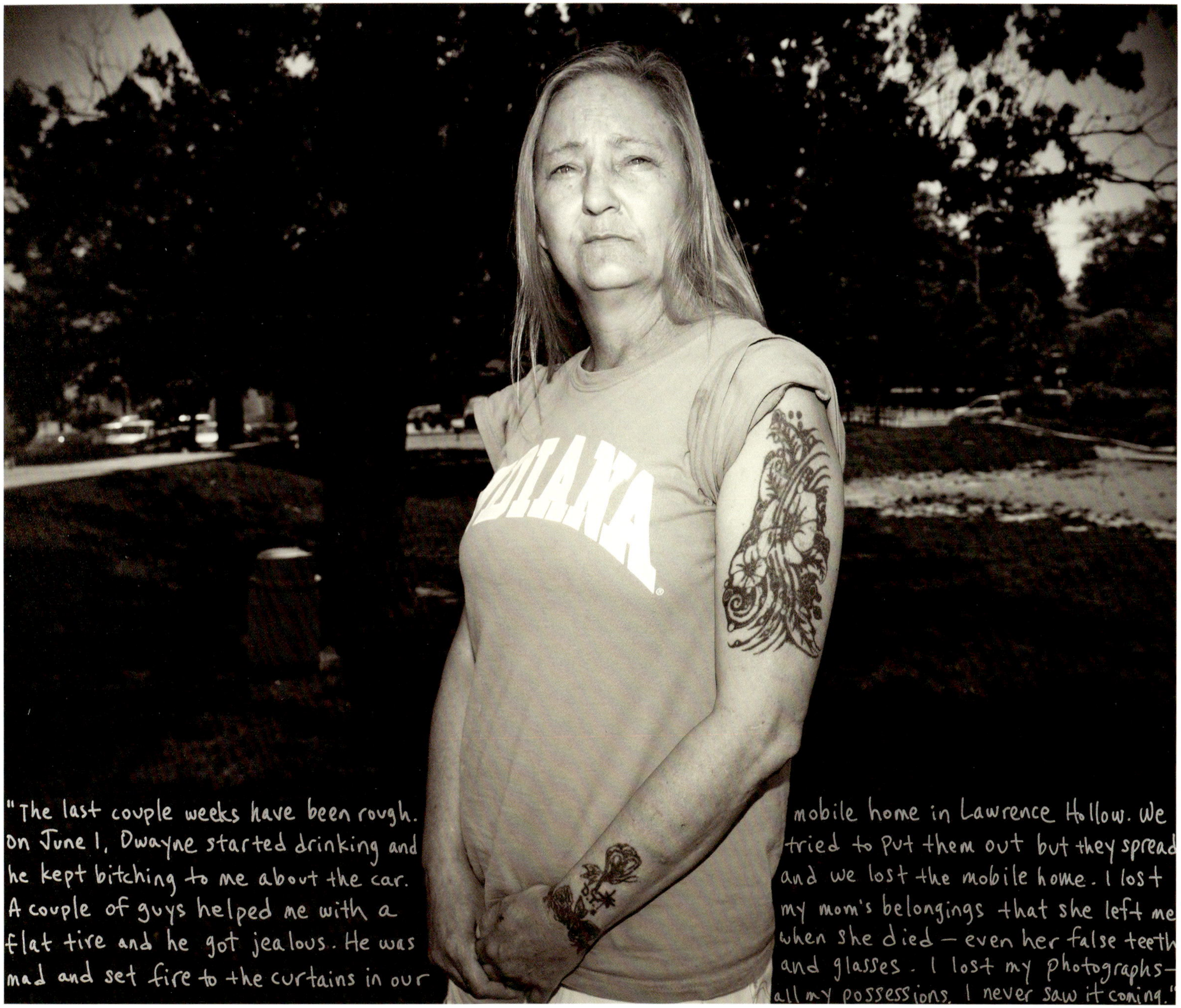

Tina after the Fire, Middle Way House, 2013

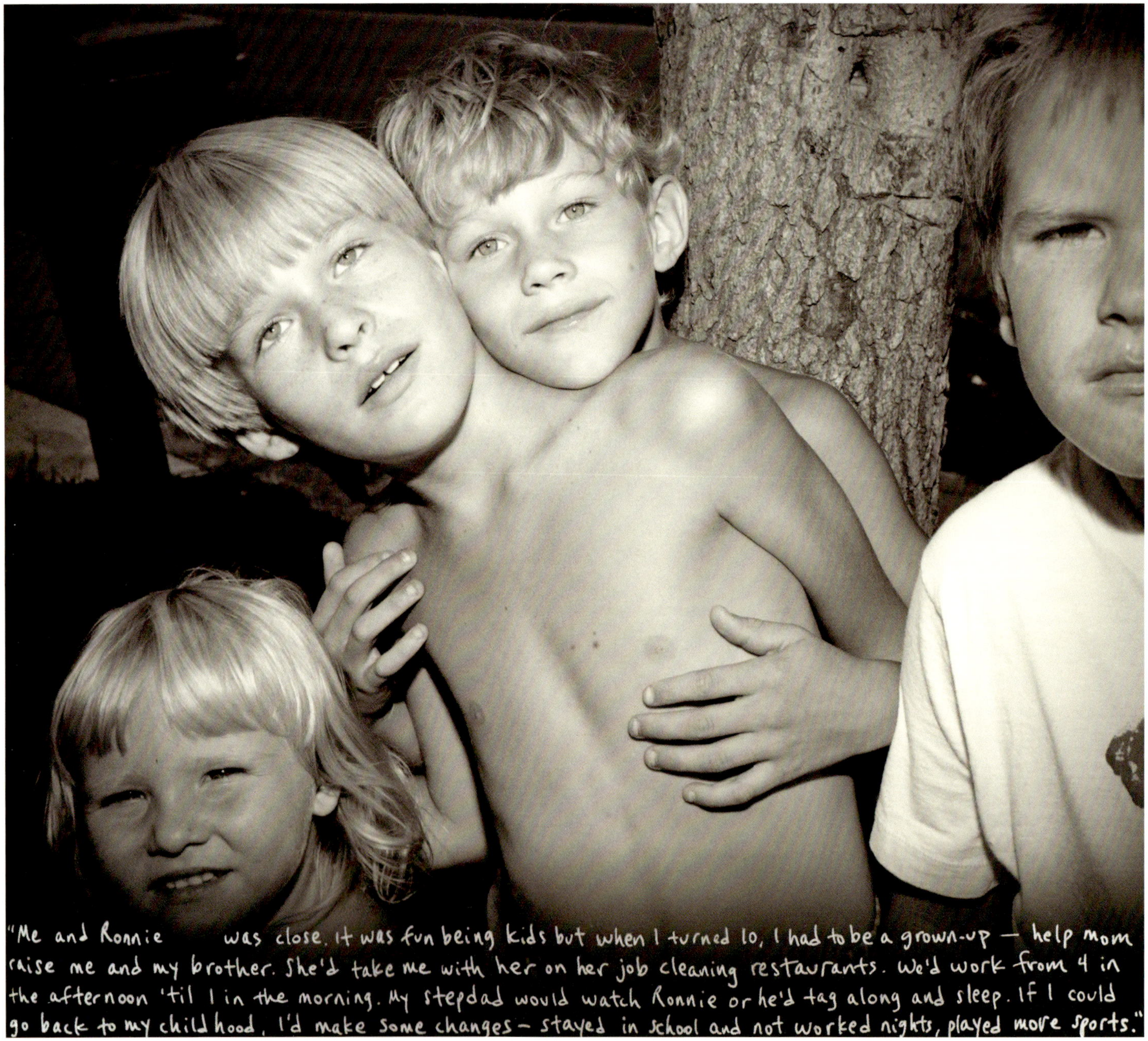

Ricky and Ronnie, Pigeon Hill, 1990

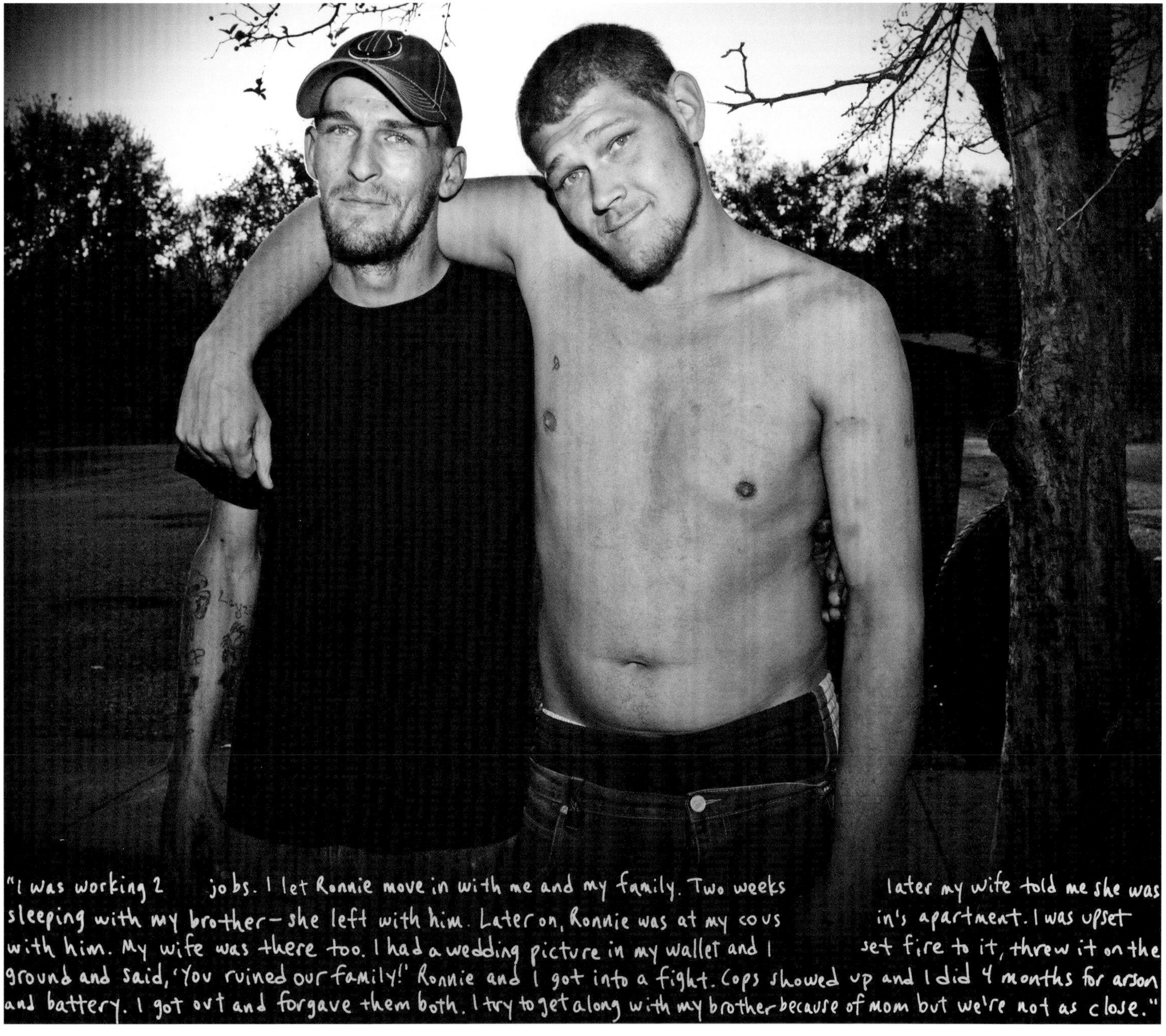

Ricky and Ronnie, Southern Winds Inn, 2011

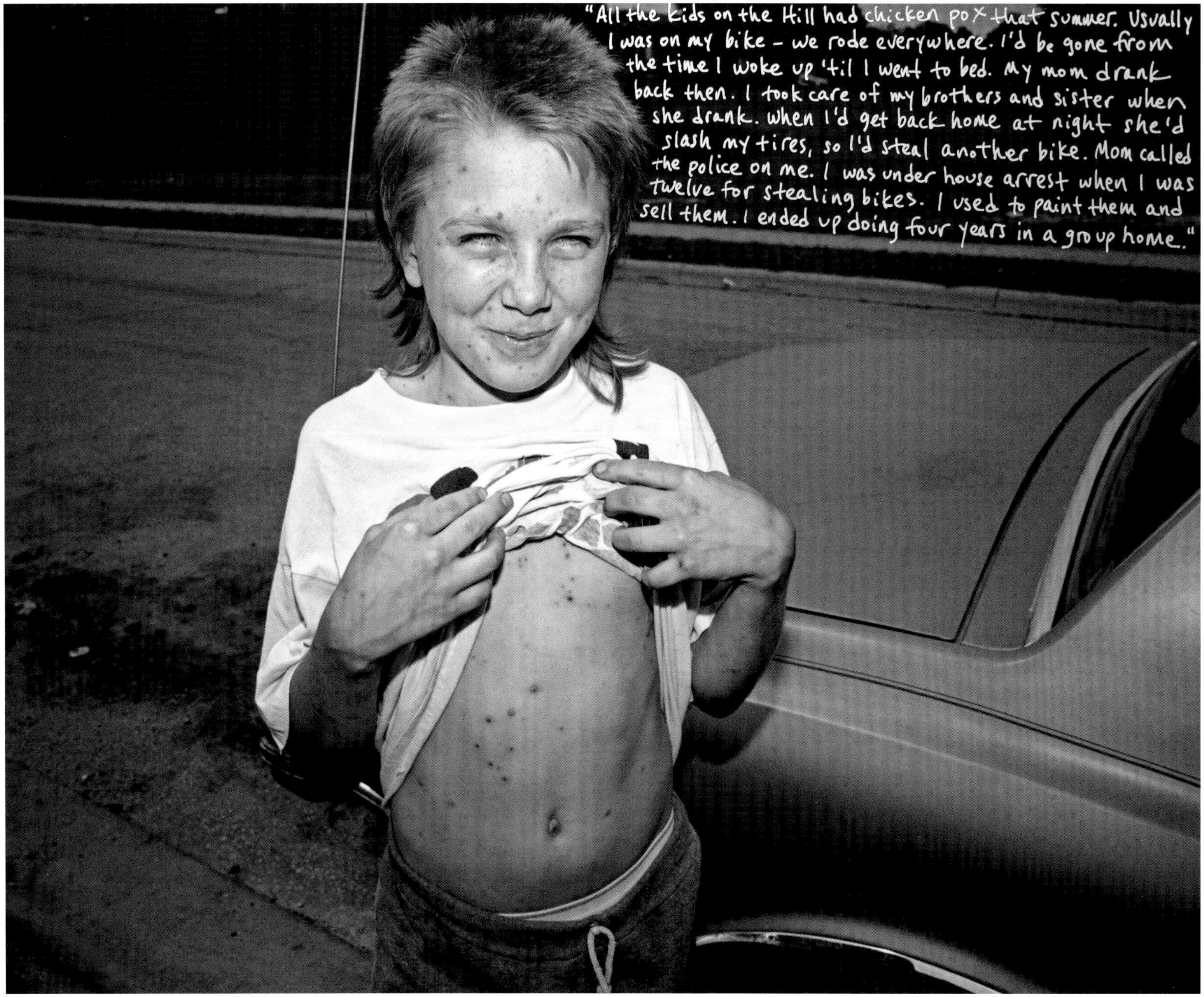

Bryan with Chicken Pox, Pigeon Hill, 1989

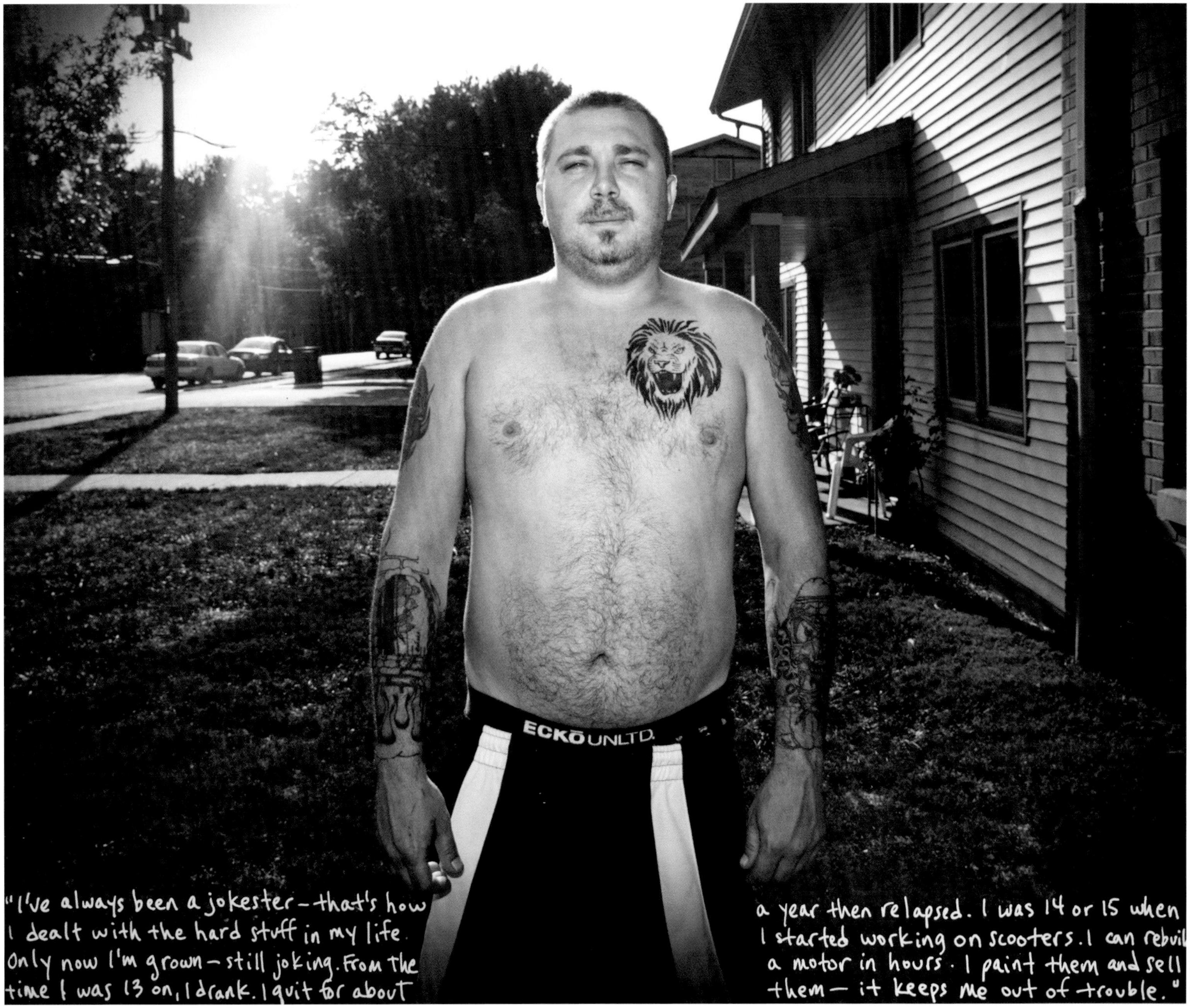

Bryan with Tattoos, Pigeon Hill, 2012

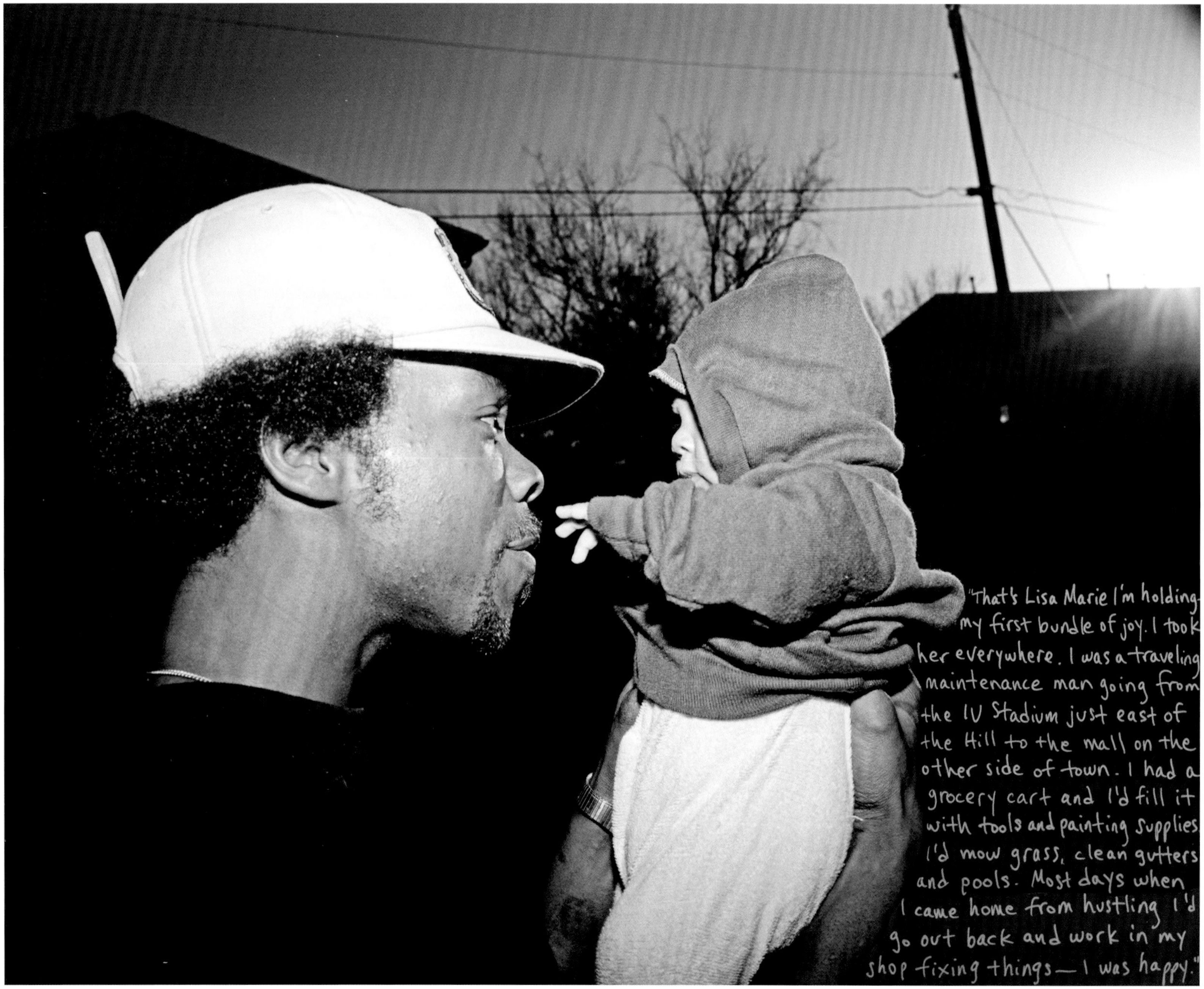

Jerrold and Oldest Daughter, Pigeon Hill, 1989

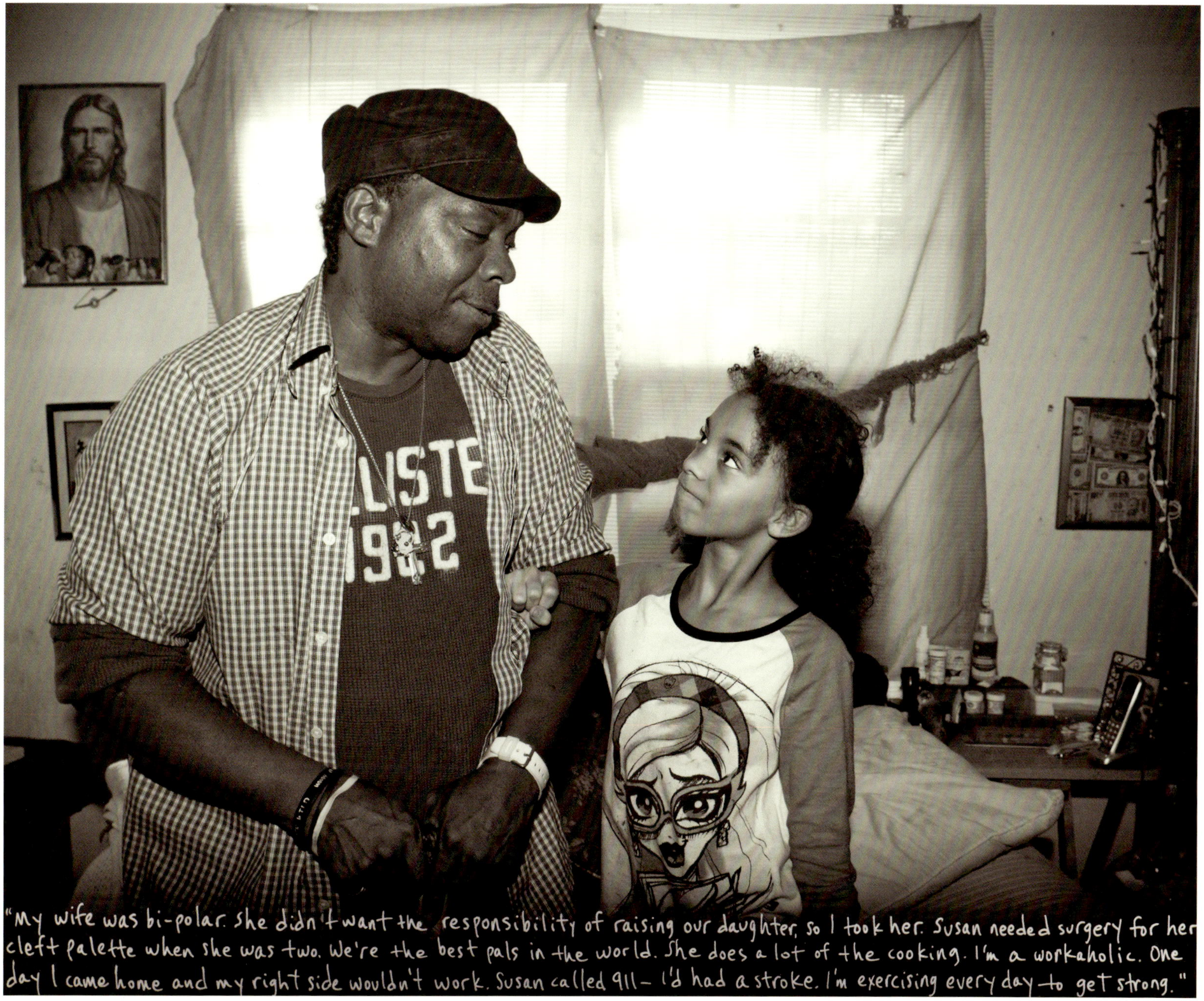

Jerrold and Youngest Daughter, 2014

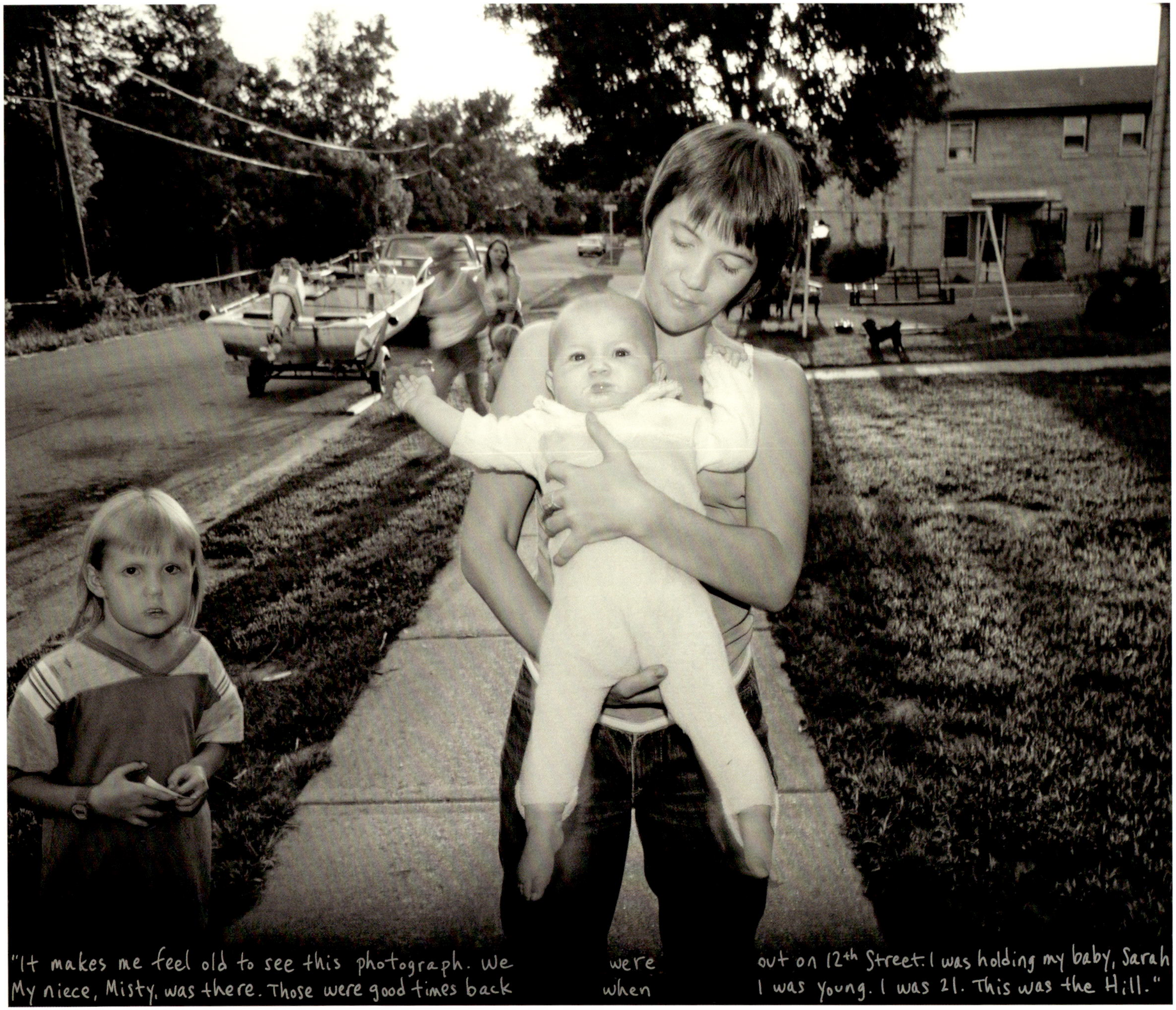

Loretta Holding Sarah as Misty Looks On, Pigeon Hill, 1989

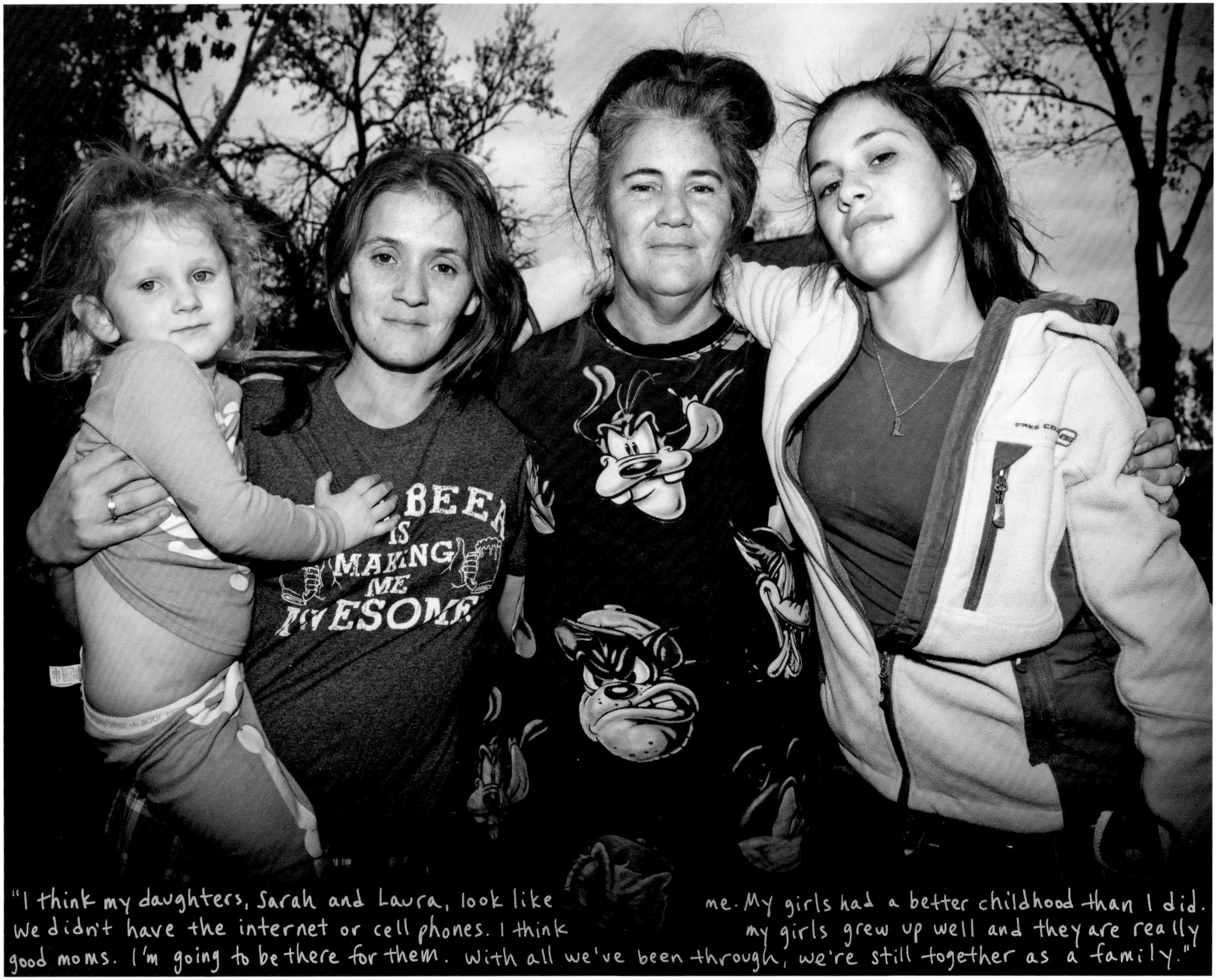

Loretta with Daughters Sarah and Laura and Granddaughter Madison, Dixie Street, 2011

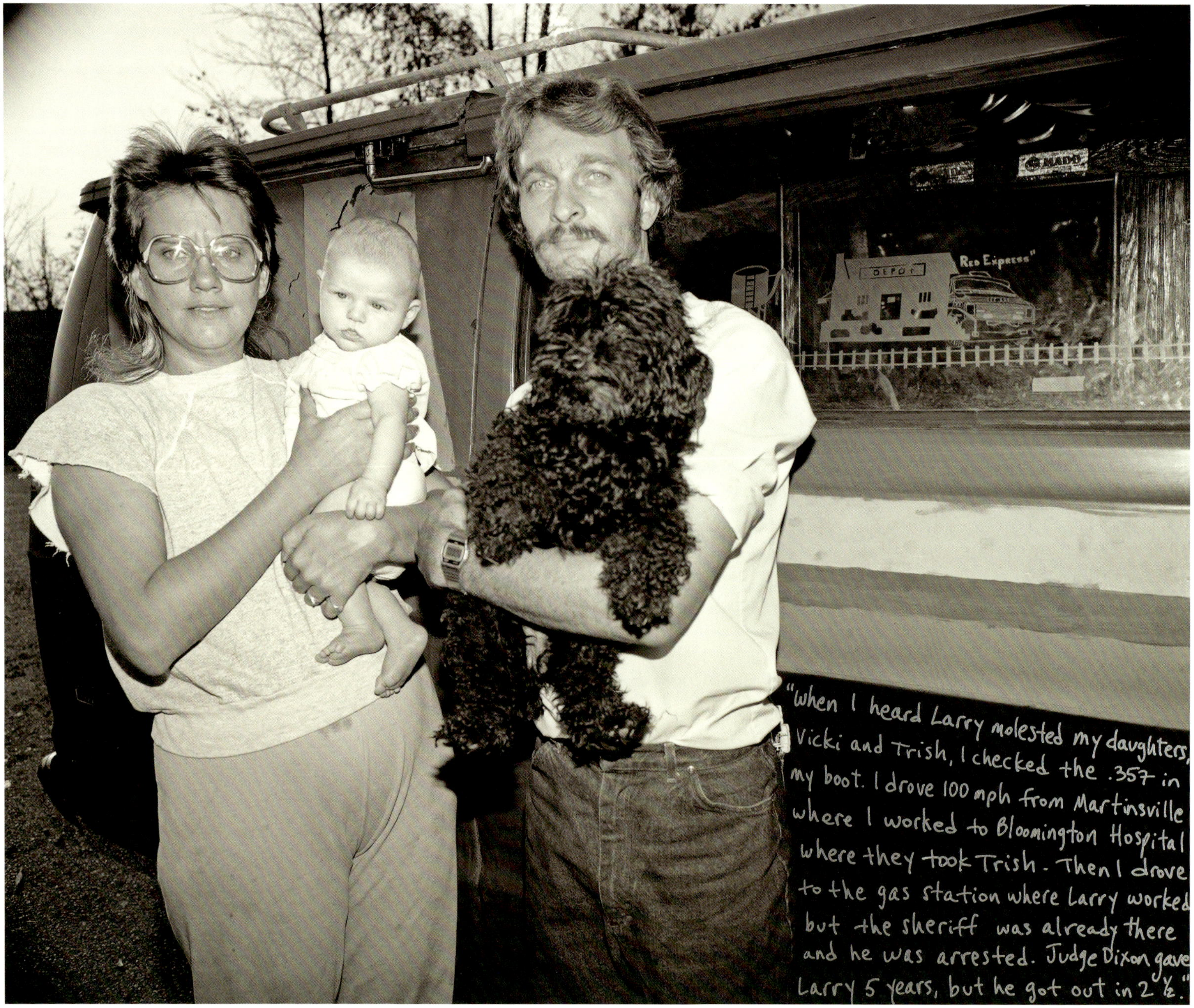

Darlene and Larry, Pigeon Hill, 1988

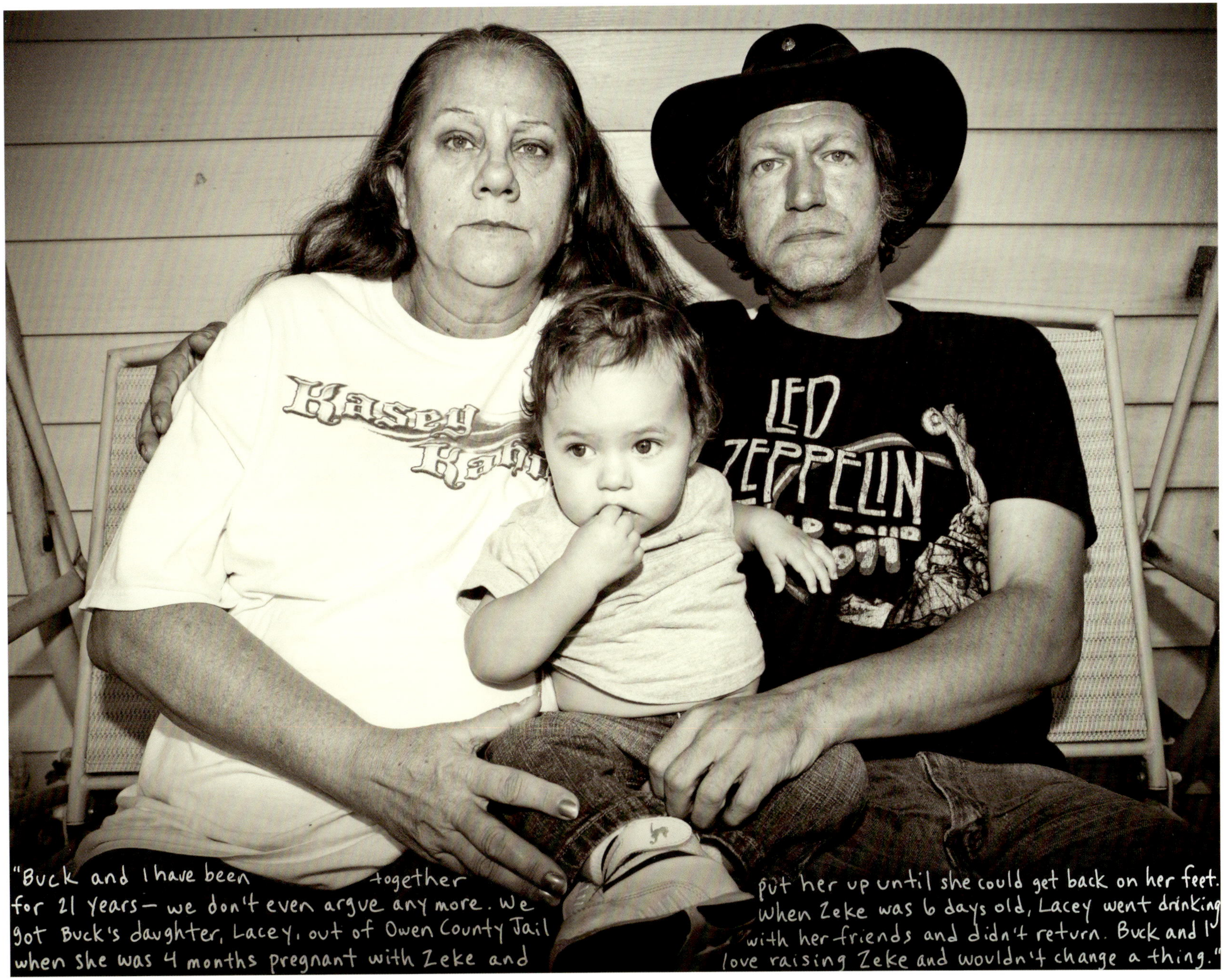

Darlene, Buck and Zeke, Spring Street, 2012

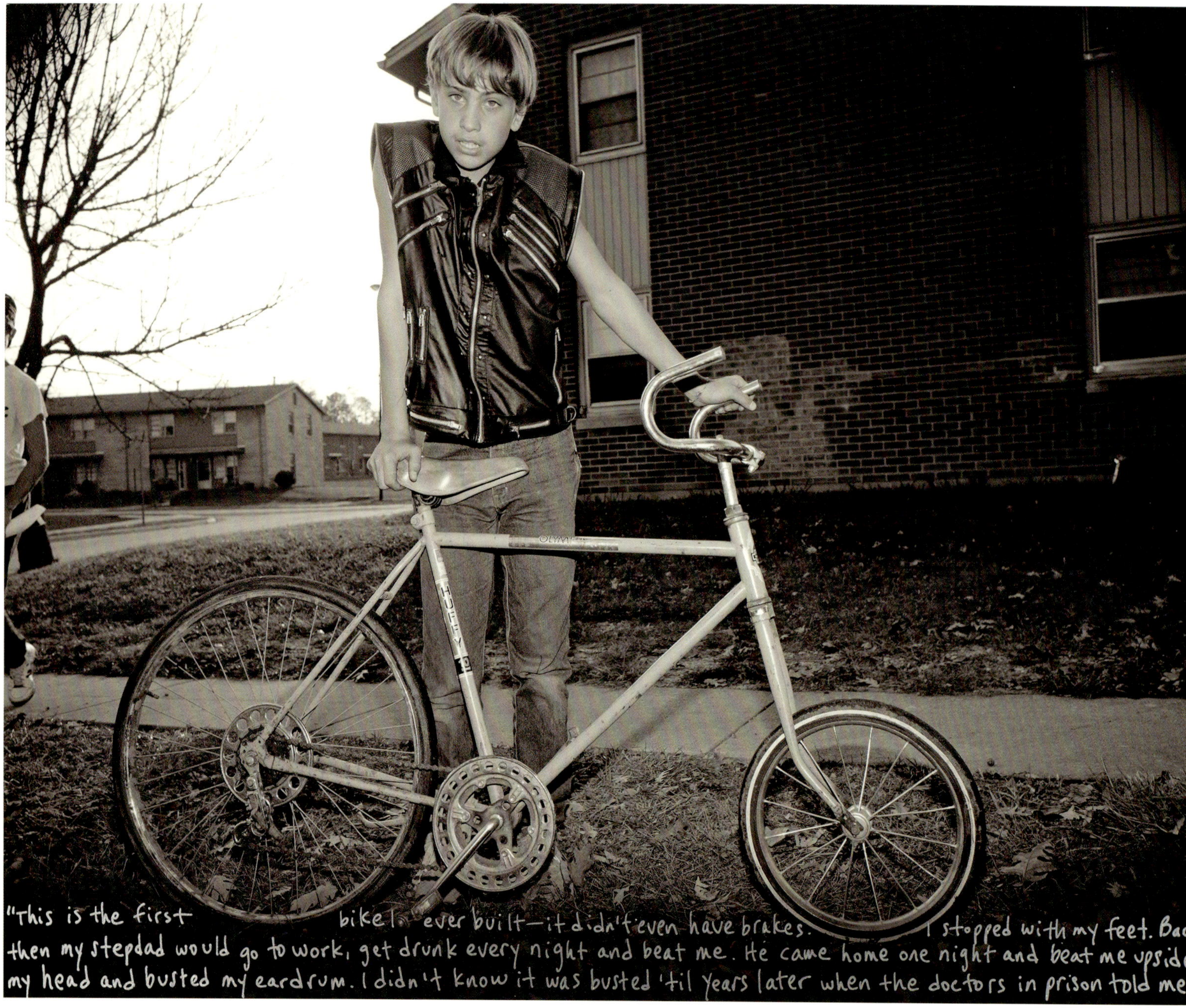

Richard and Bike, Pigeon Hill, 1989

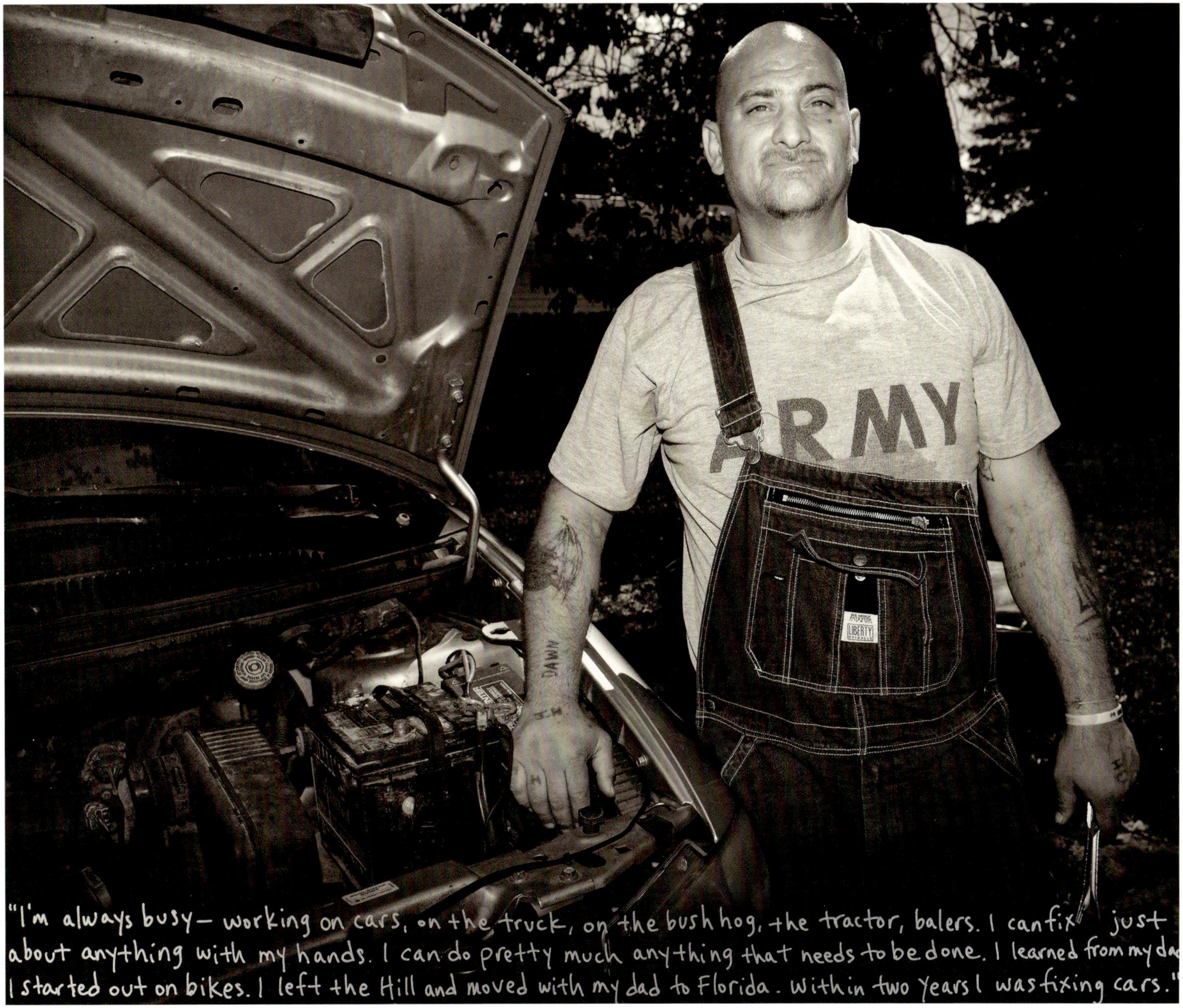

Richard Fixing Van, West Side, 2013

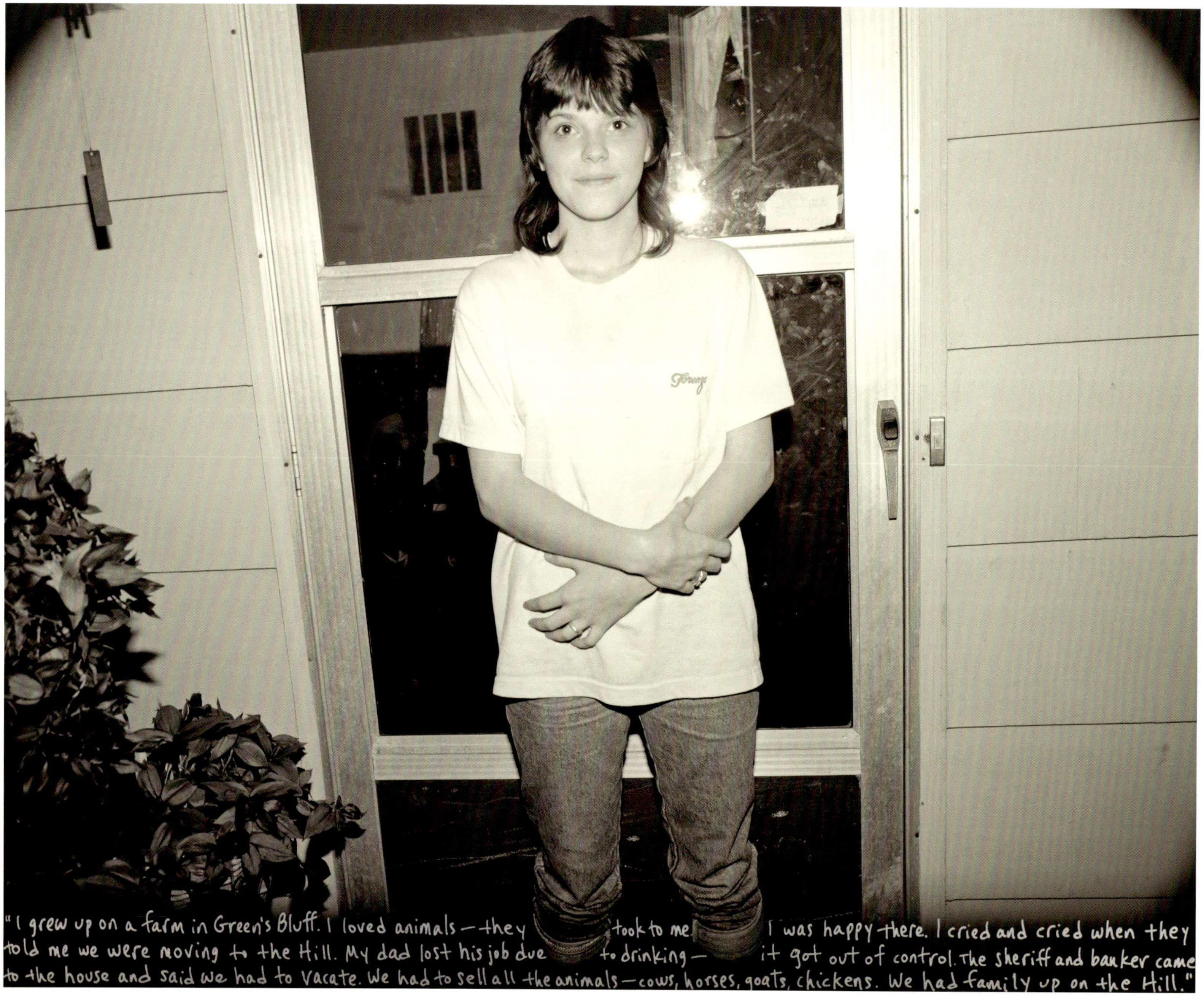

Kimberly, Pigeon Hill, 1989

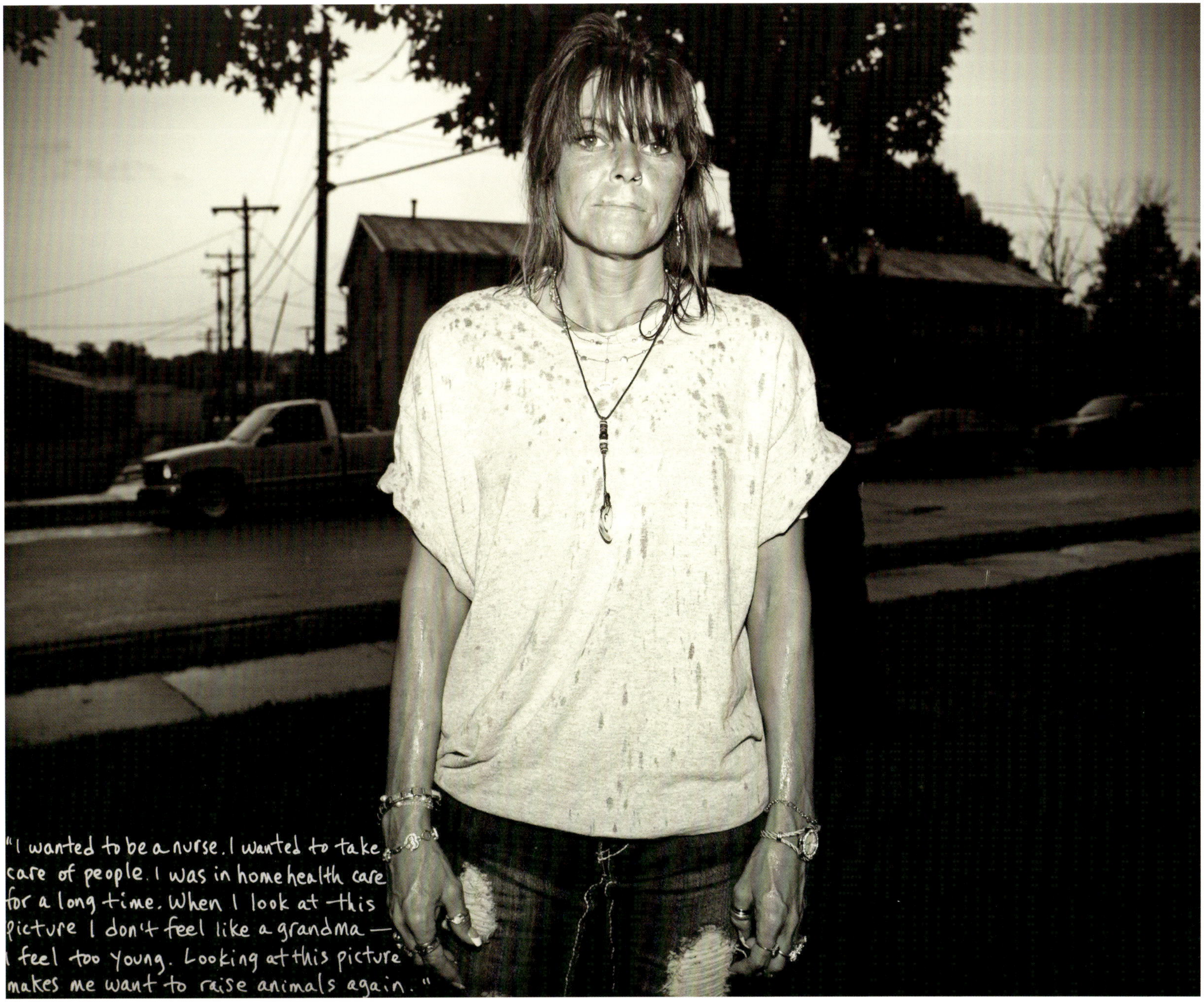

Kimberly at Daughter's Apartment, Pigeon Hill, 2013

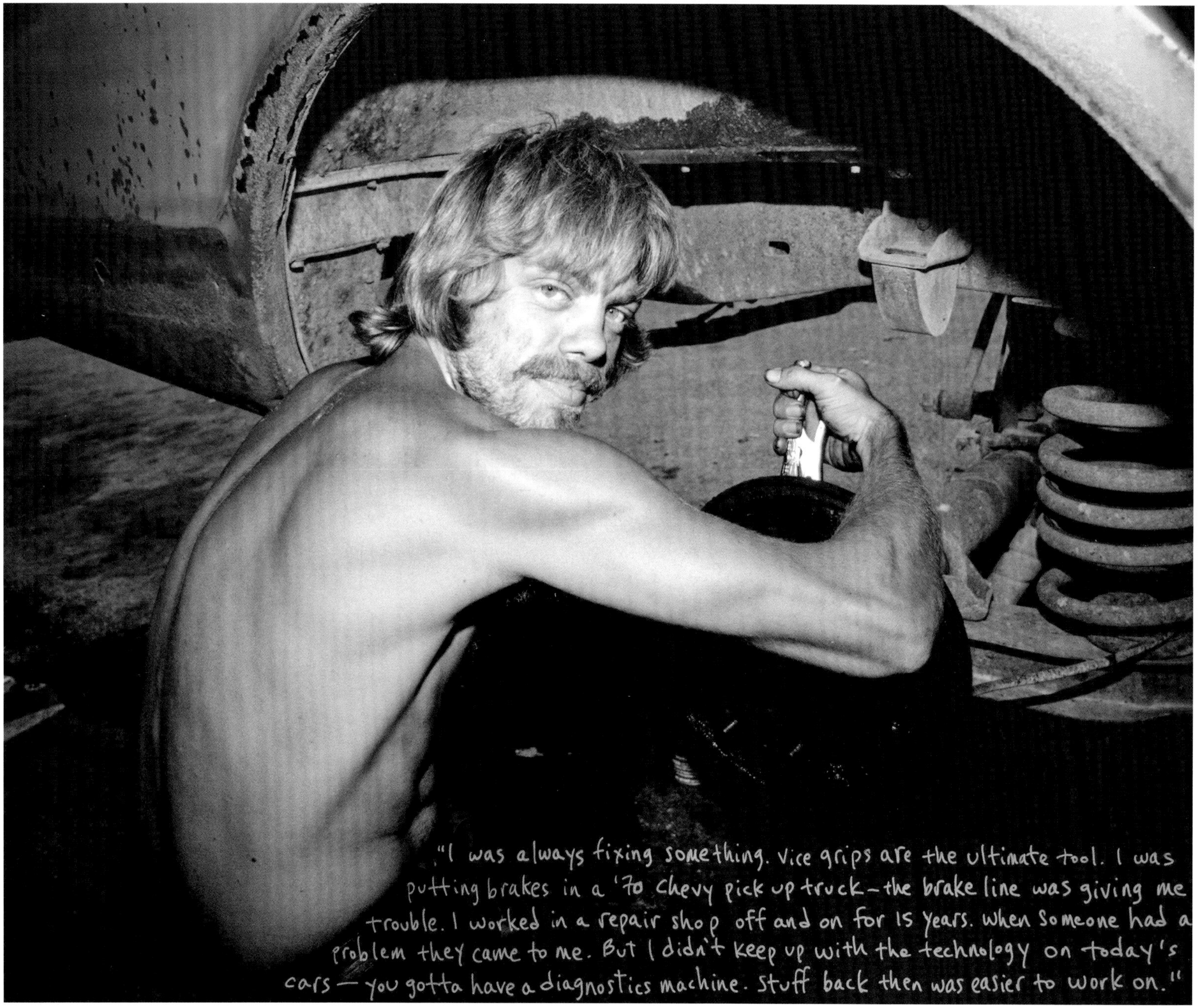

Marvin Sr. Fixing Brakes, Pigeon Hill, 1991

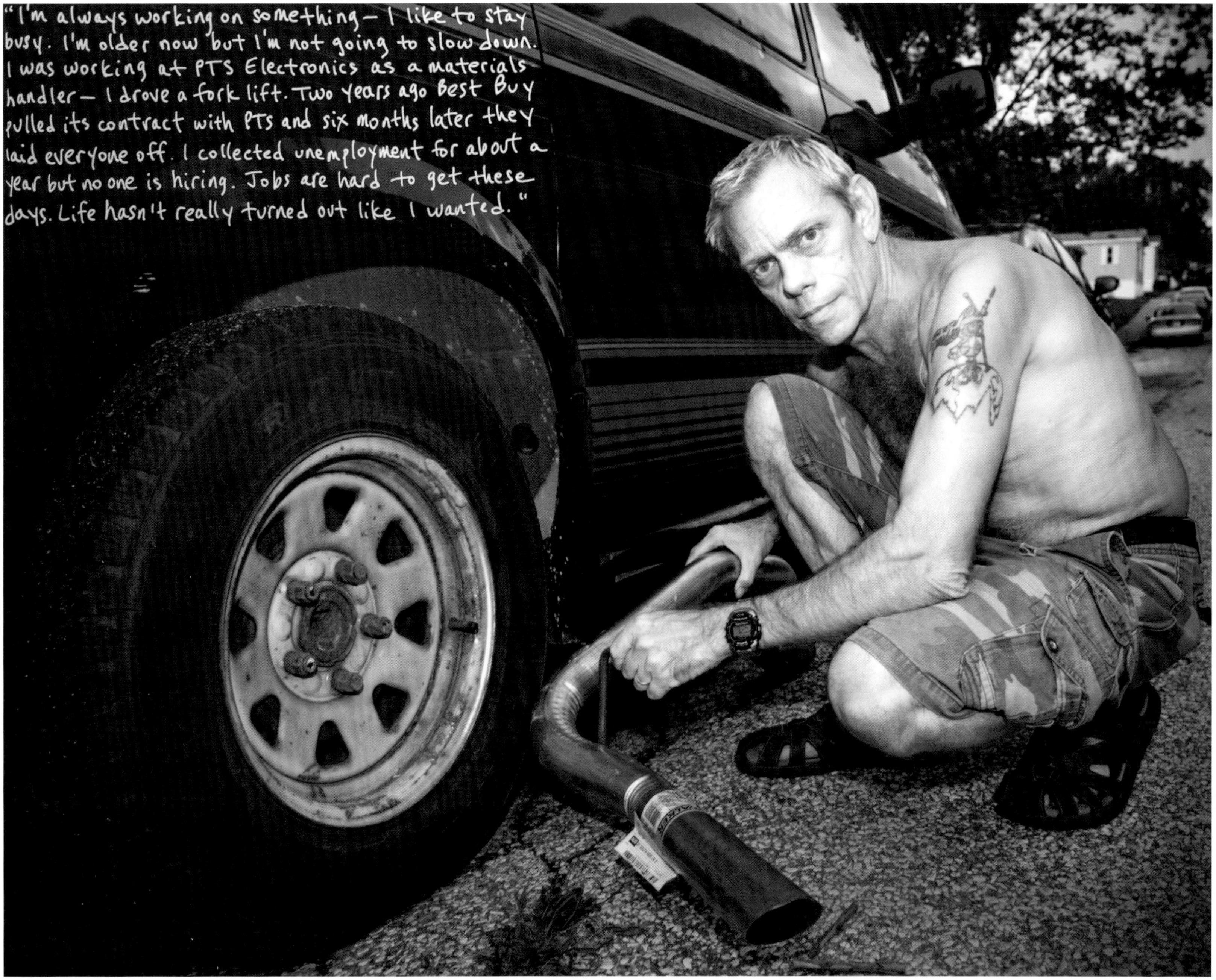

Marvin Sr., Arlington Valley Mobile Park, 2014

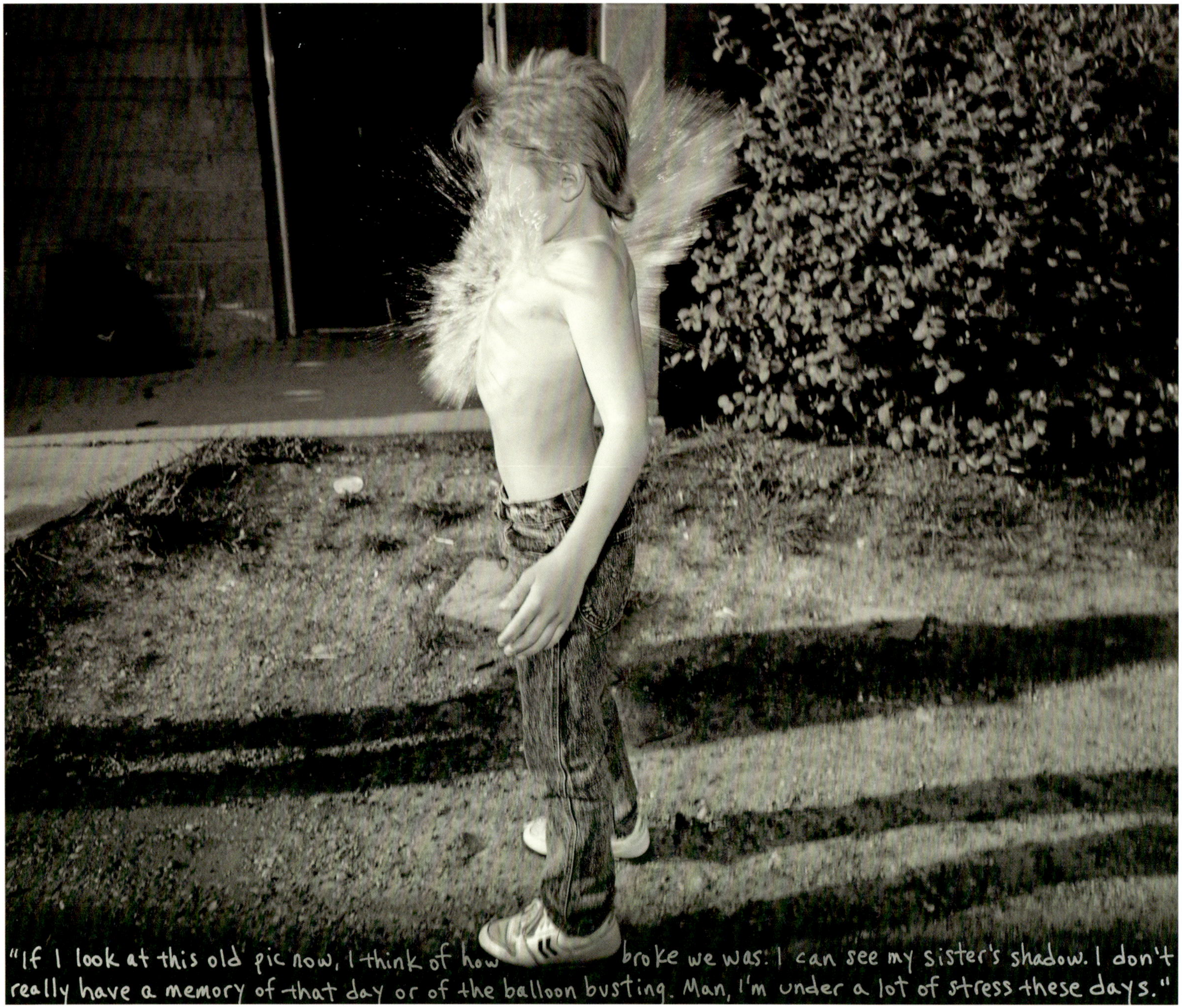

Stevie and the Water Balloon, Pigeon Hill, 1988

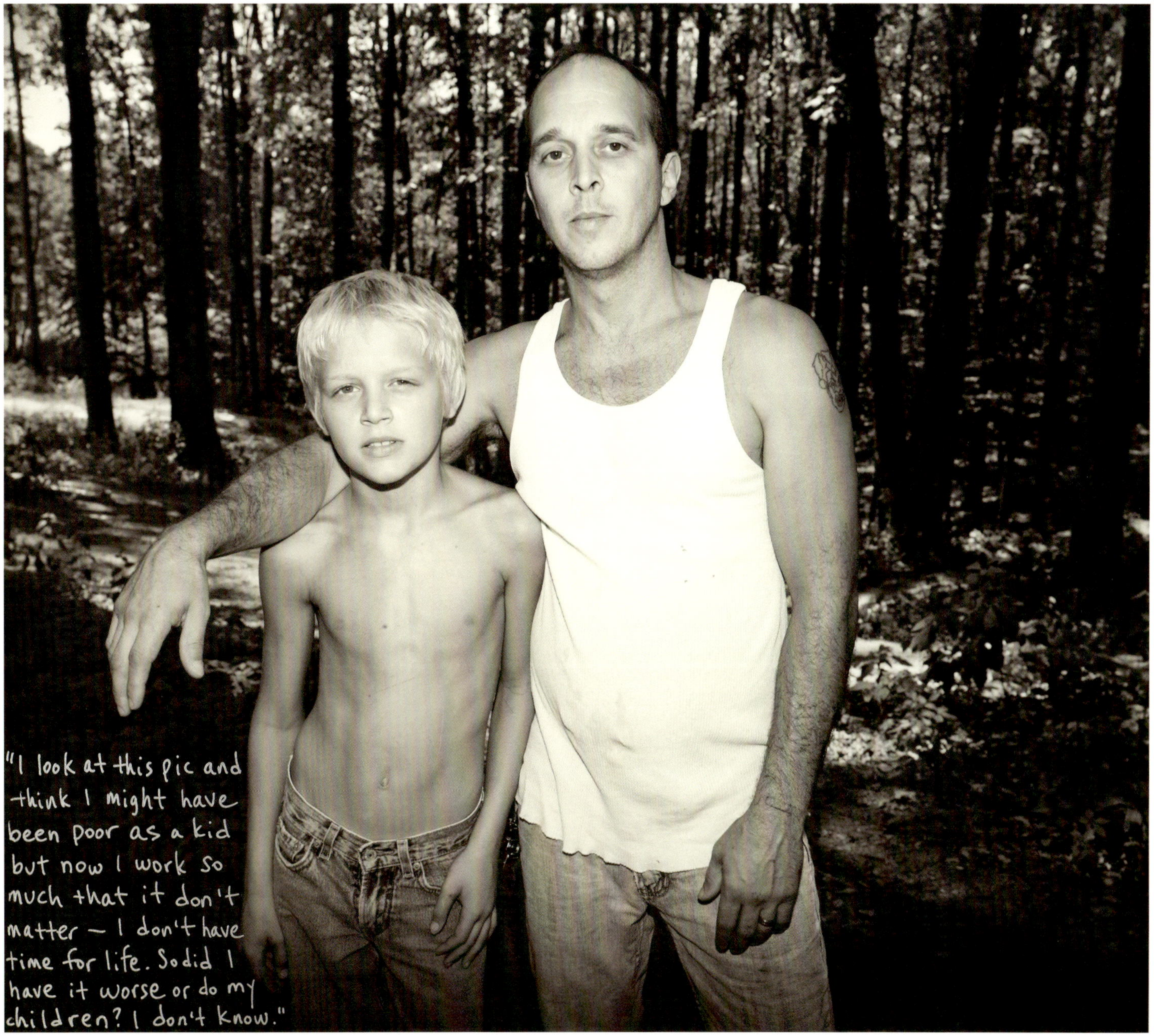

Steve and Son, County Line Road, 2012

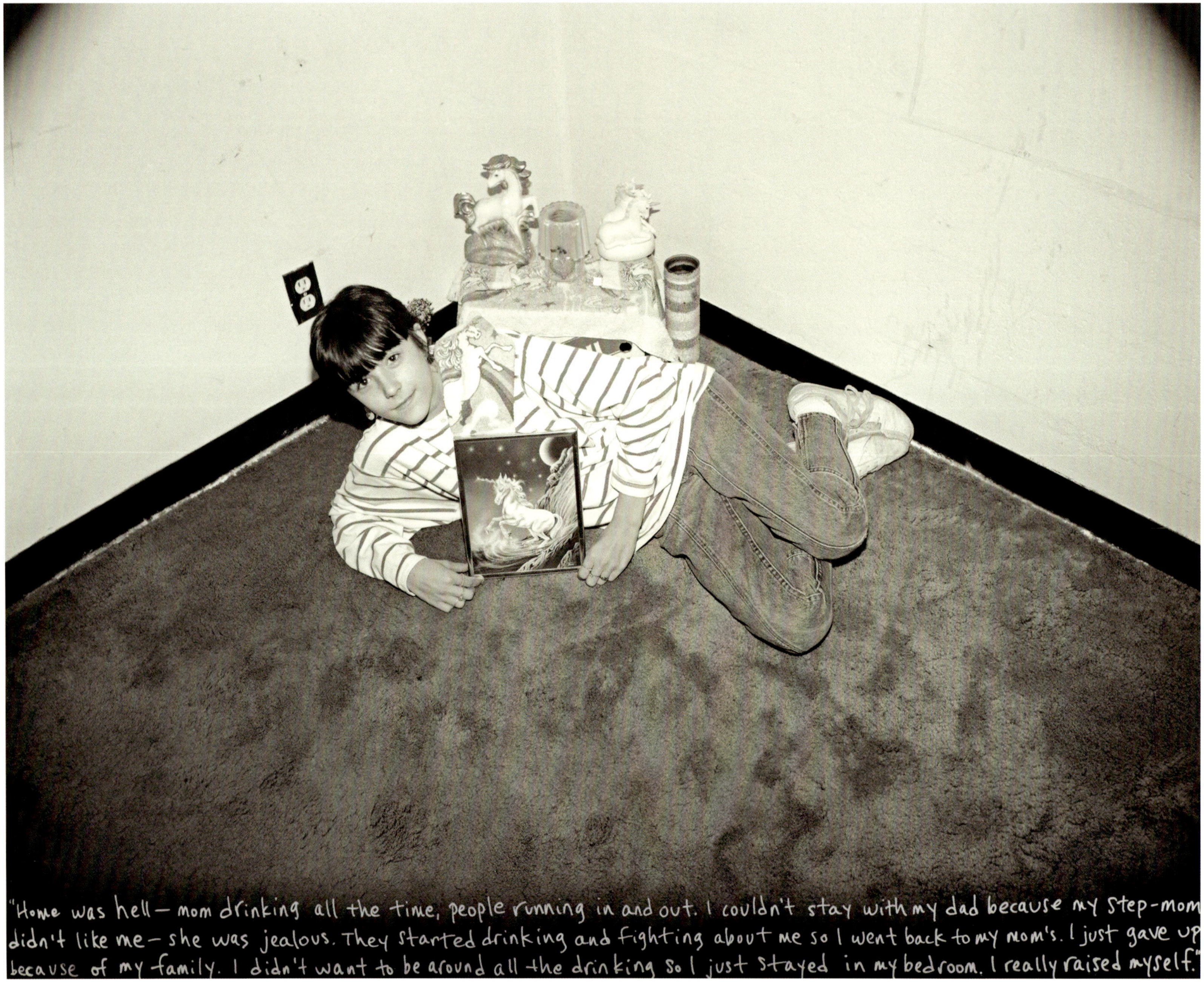

Crystal with Unicorns, Pigeon Hill, 1989

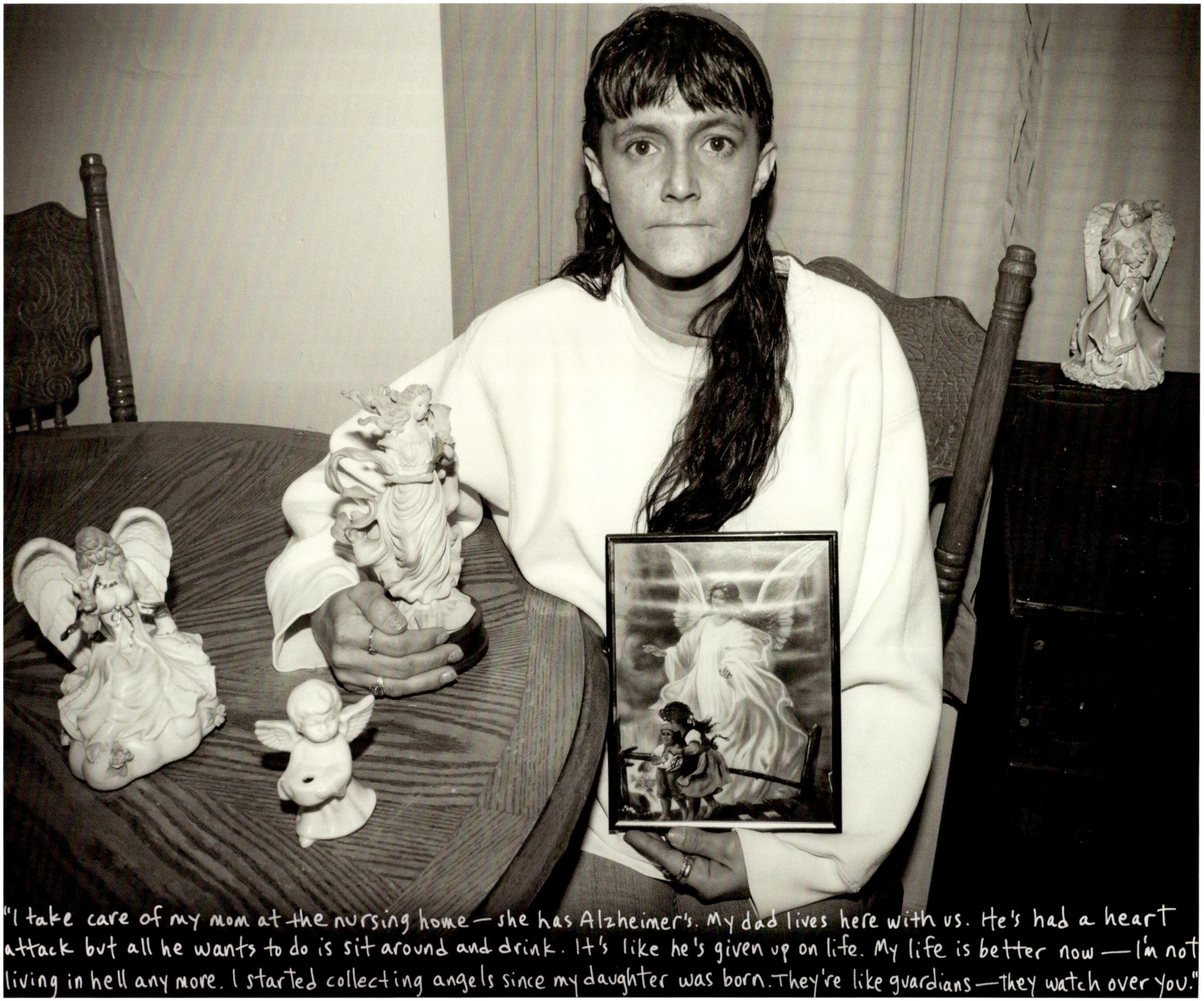

Crystal with Angels, Pigeon Hill, 2014

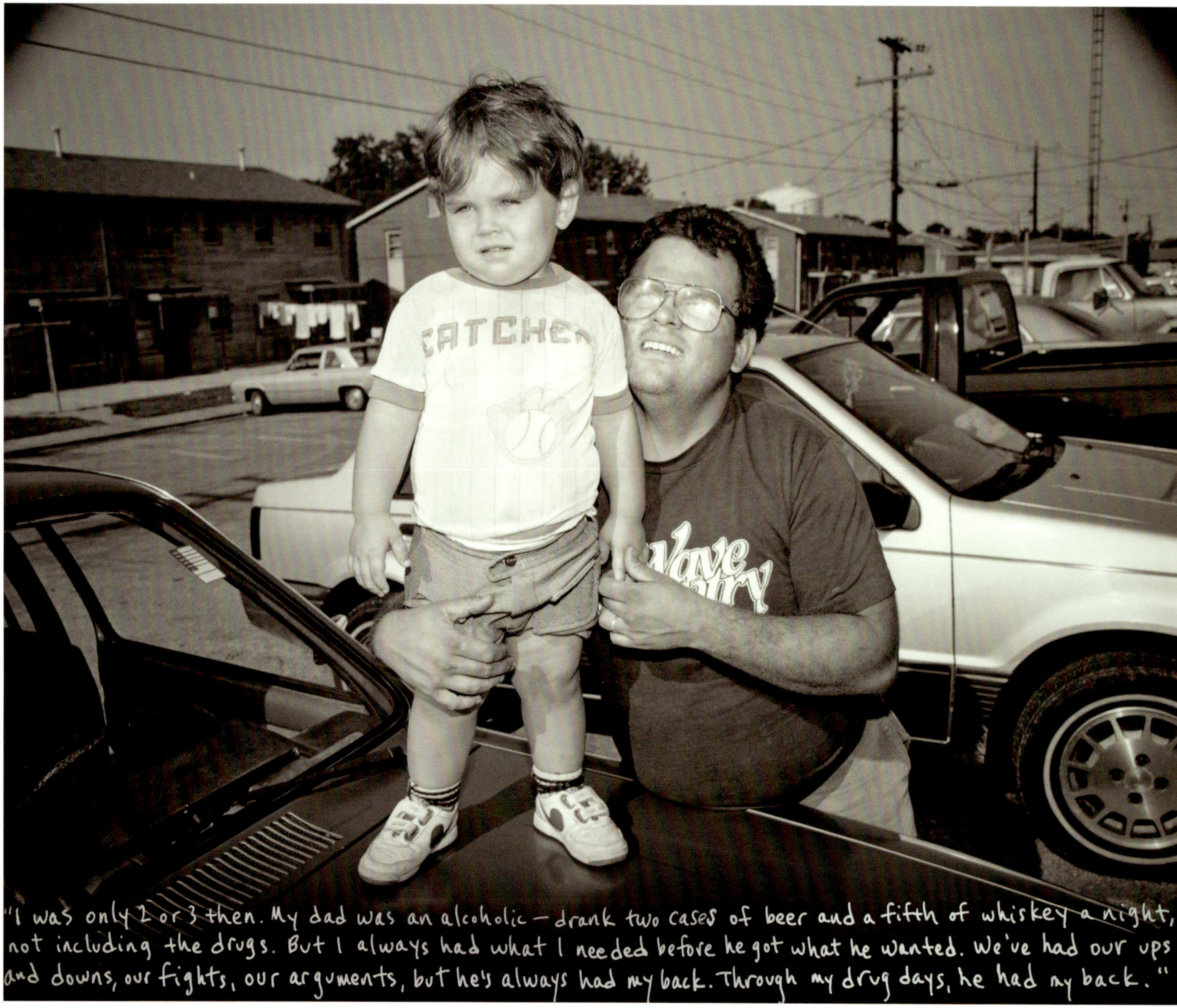

Carl with his Father, Pigeon Hill, 1990

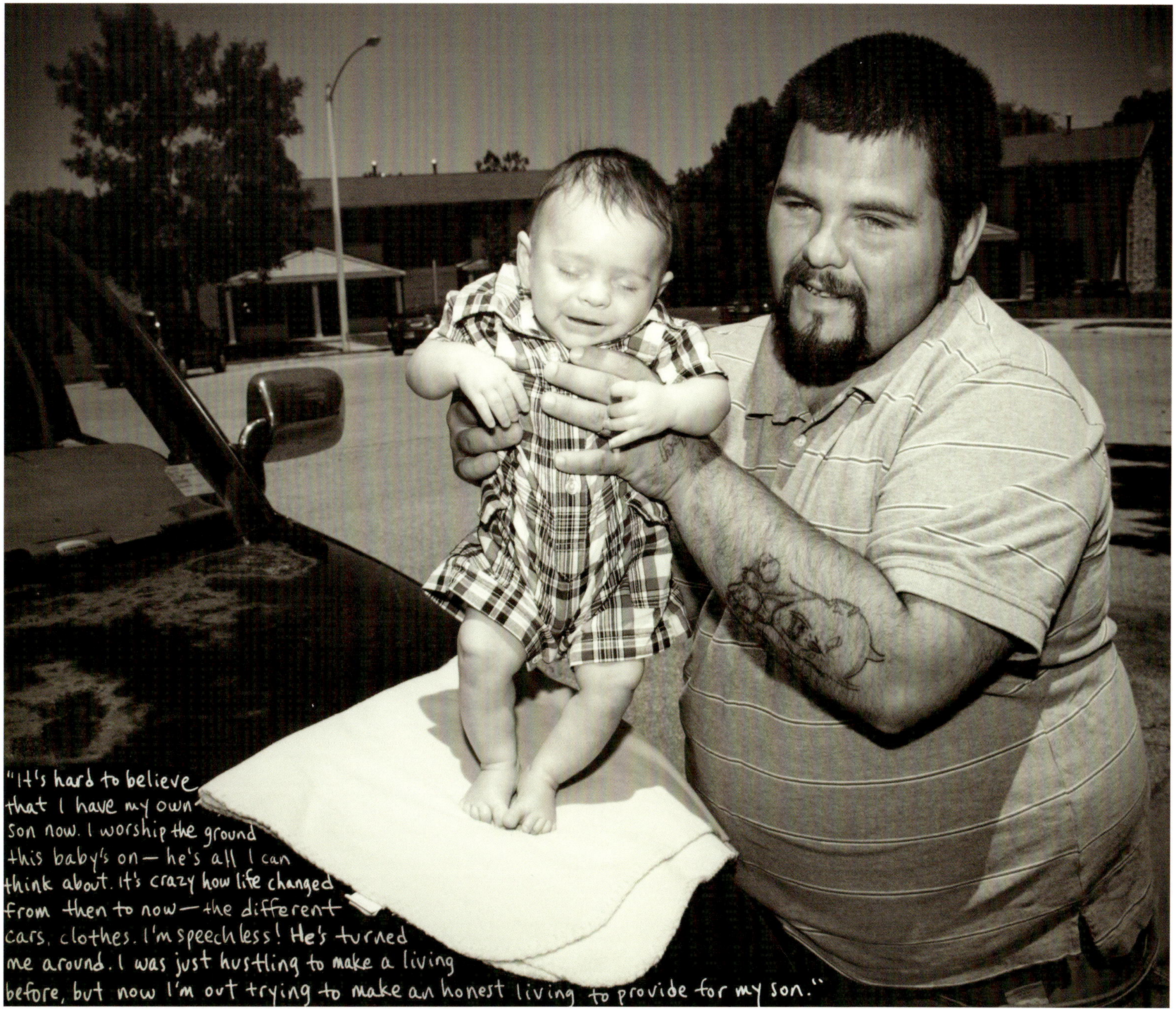

Carl with his Son, Pigeon Hill, 2014

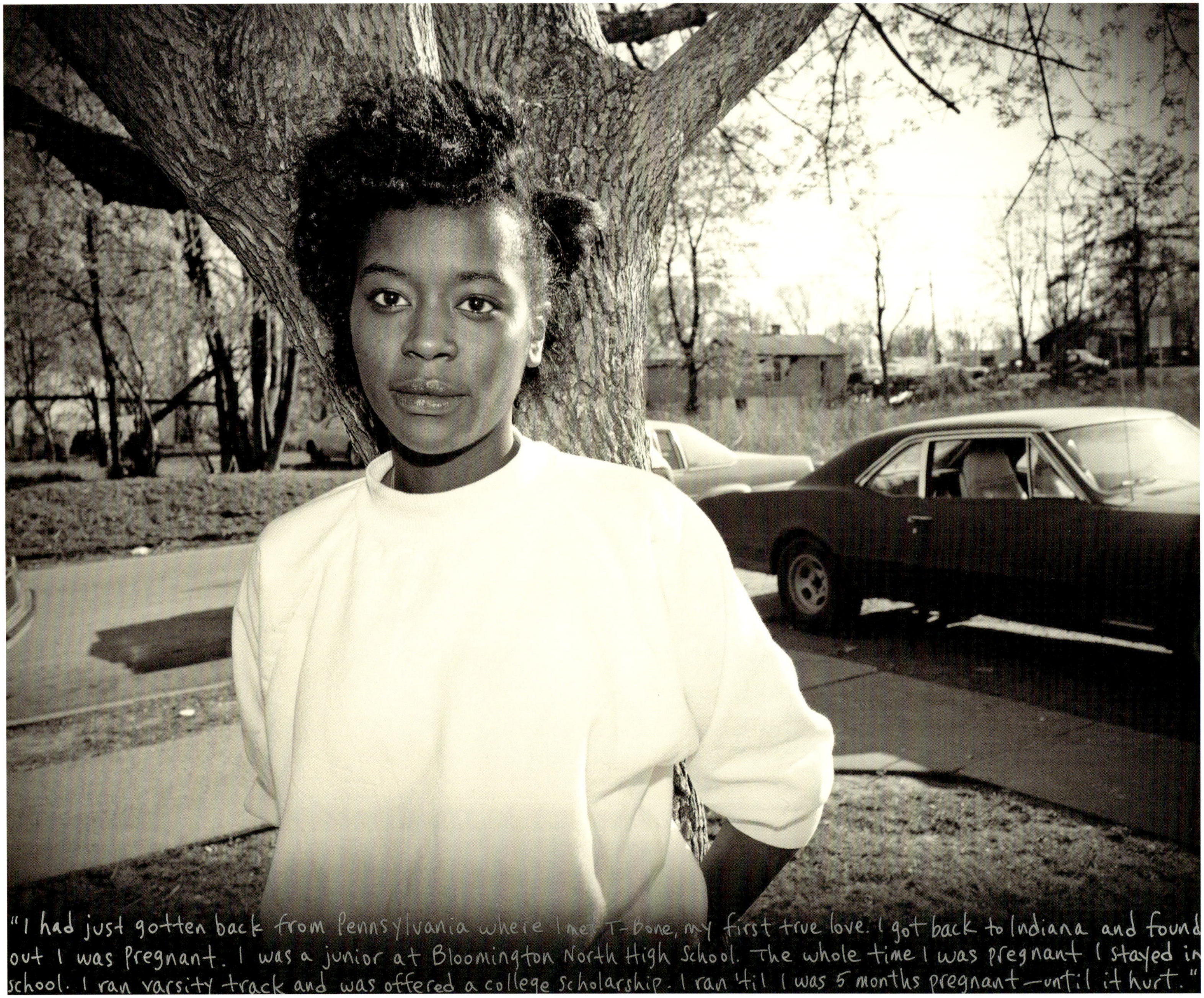

Kym, Pigeon Hill, 1988

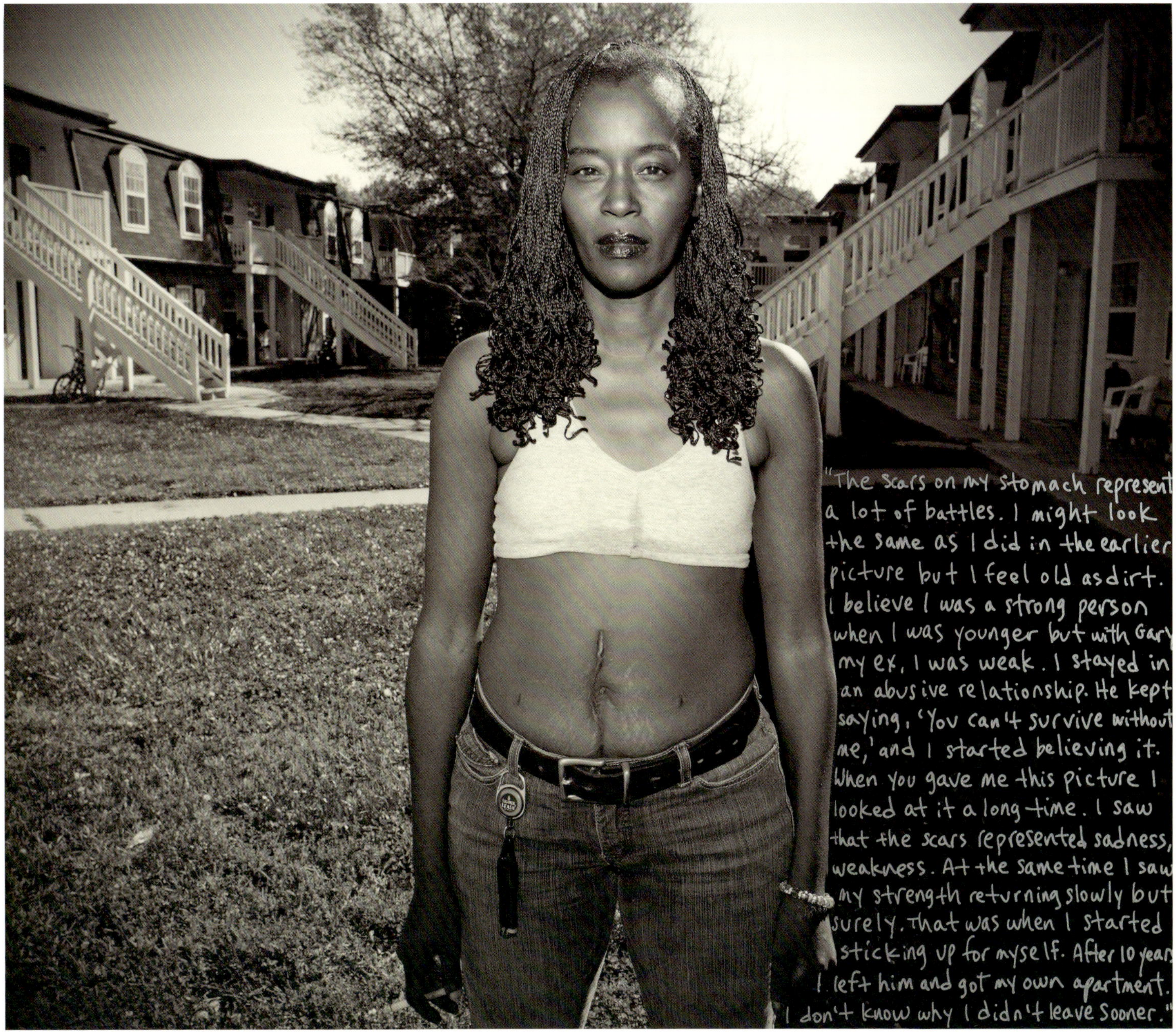

Kym with Caesarean Scar, Woodland Springs Apartments, 2011

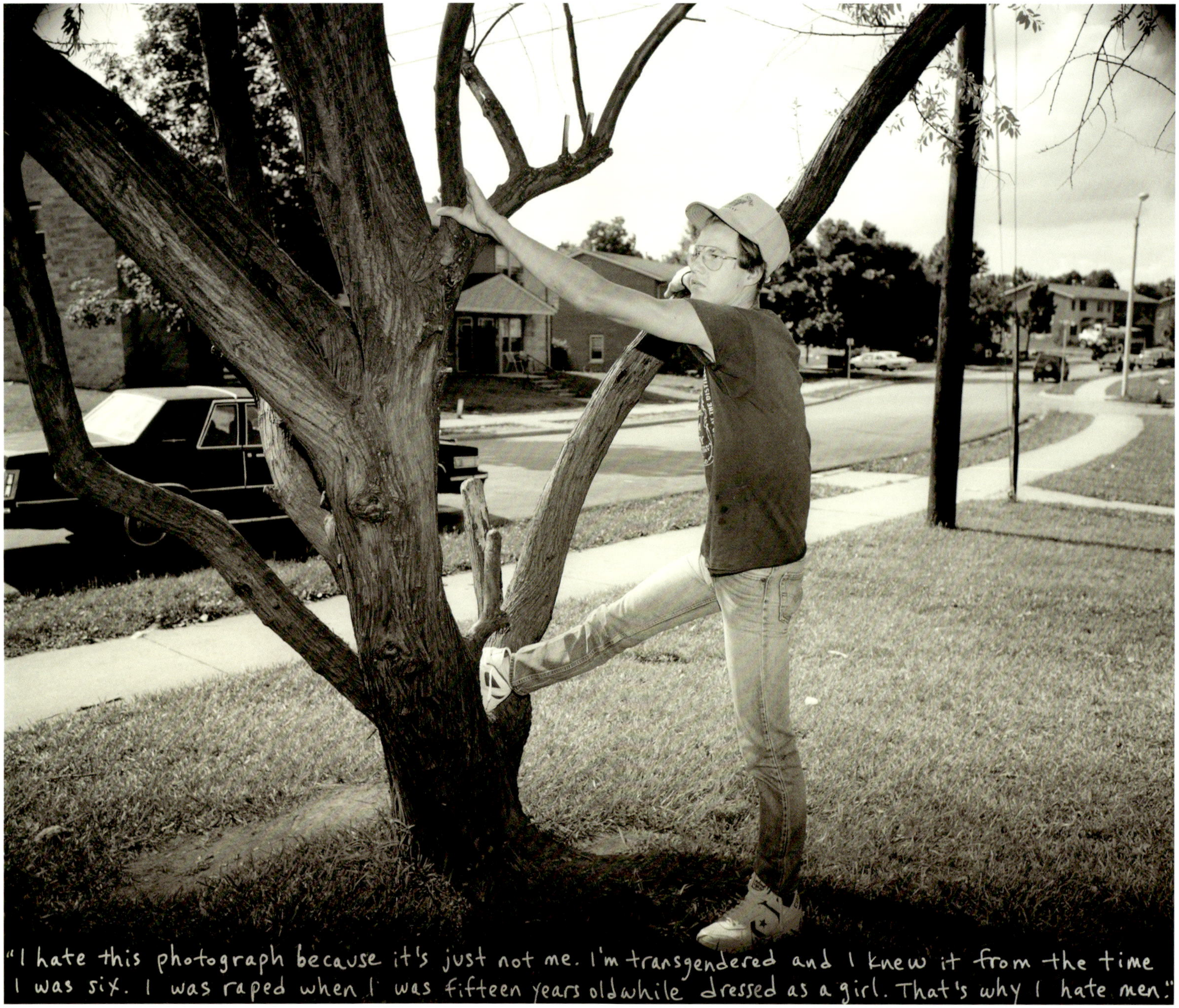

Junior, Pigeon Hill, 1990

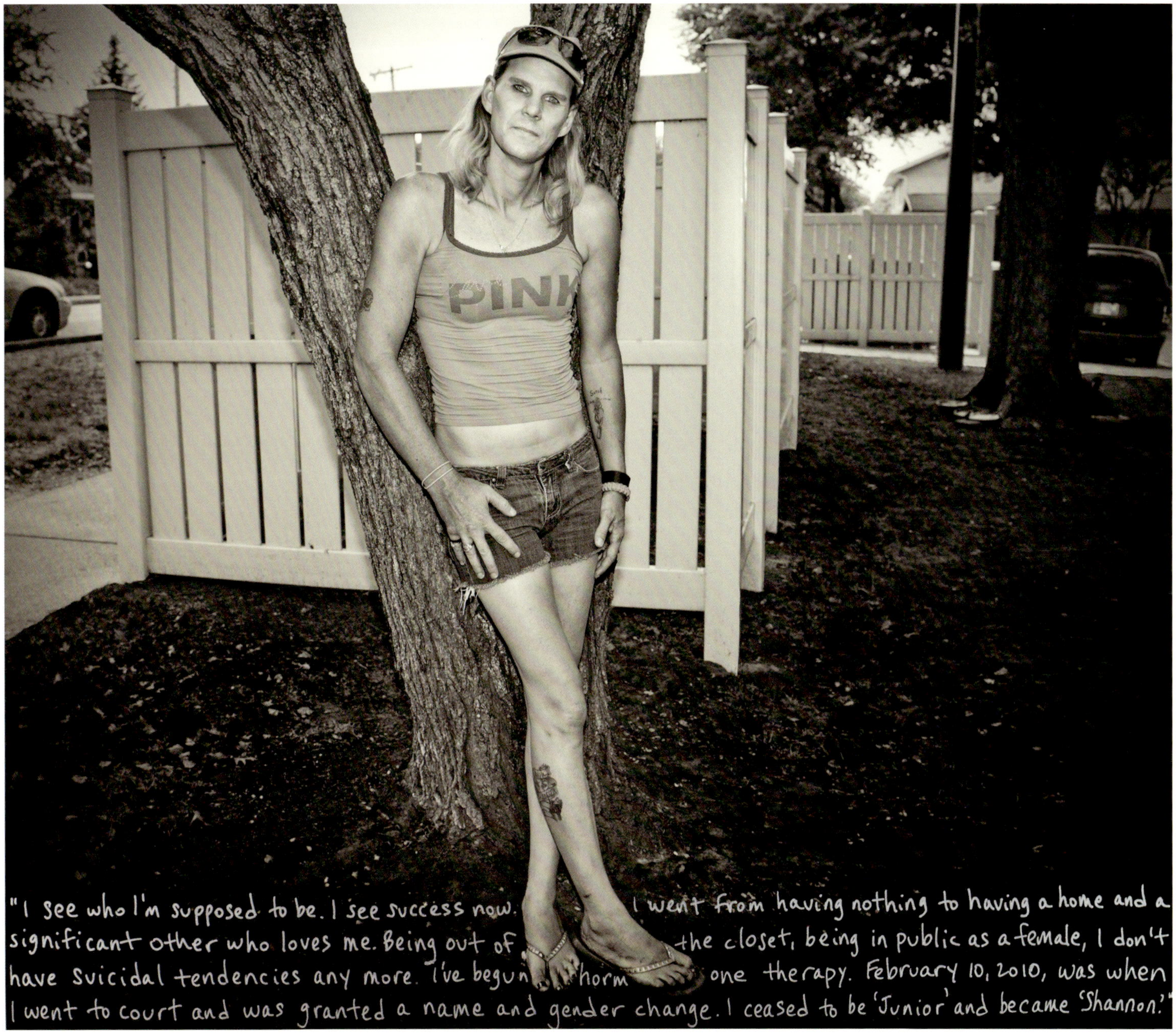

Shannon after Gender Change, Pigeon Hill, 2012

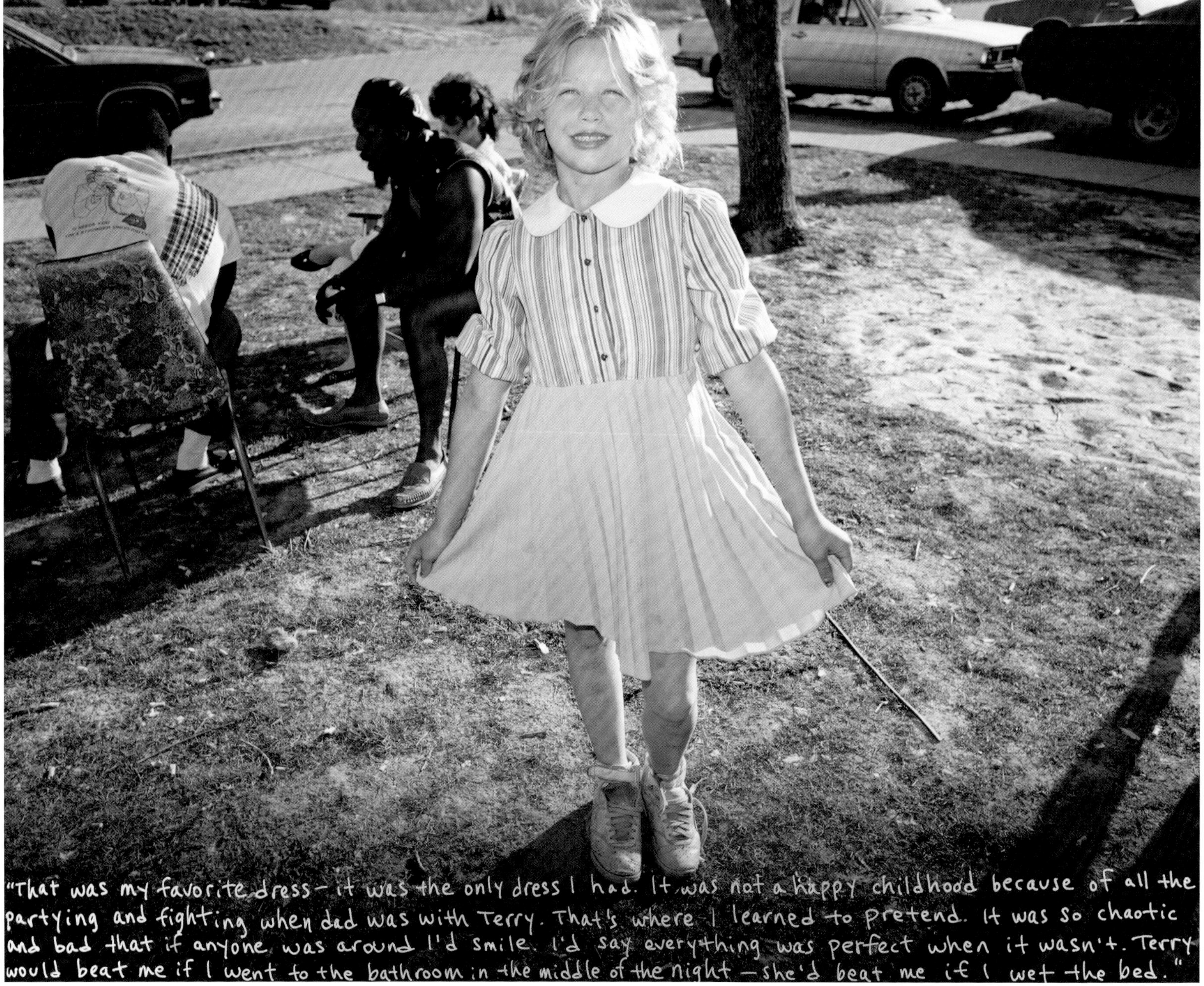

Jamie's Only Dress, Pigeon Hill, 1988

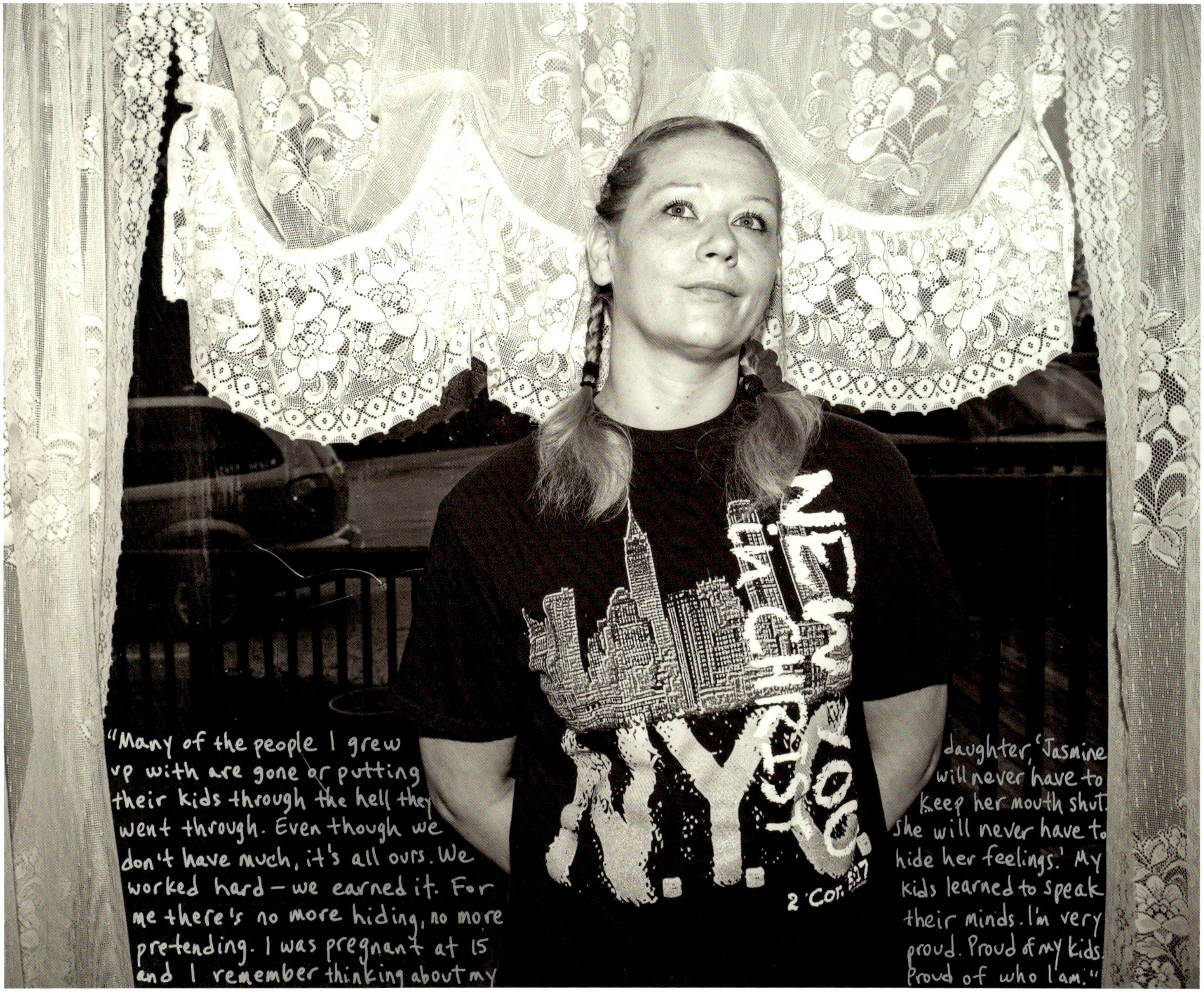

Jamie, Greene County, 2013

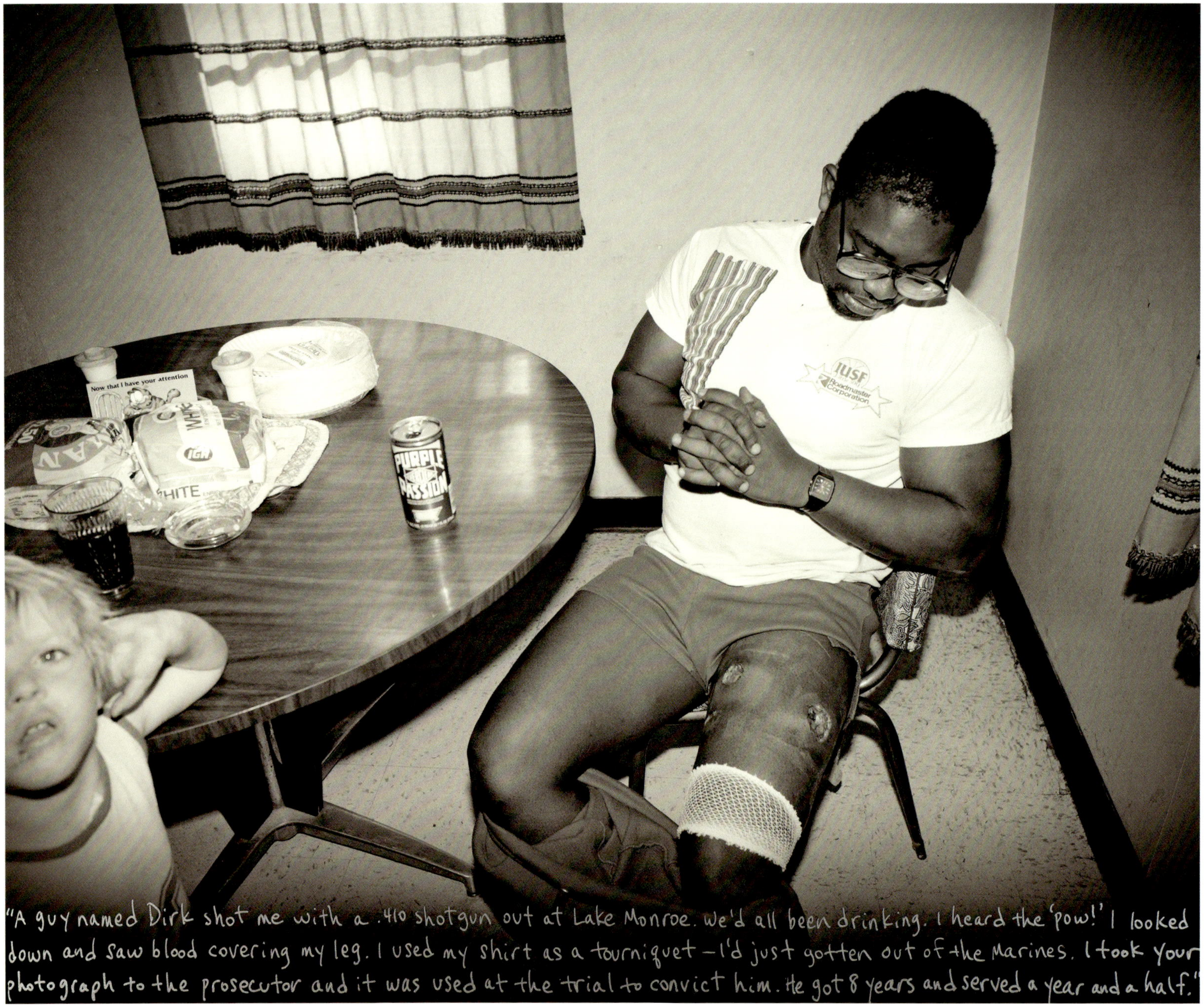

Kevin is Shot, Pigeon Hill, 1988

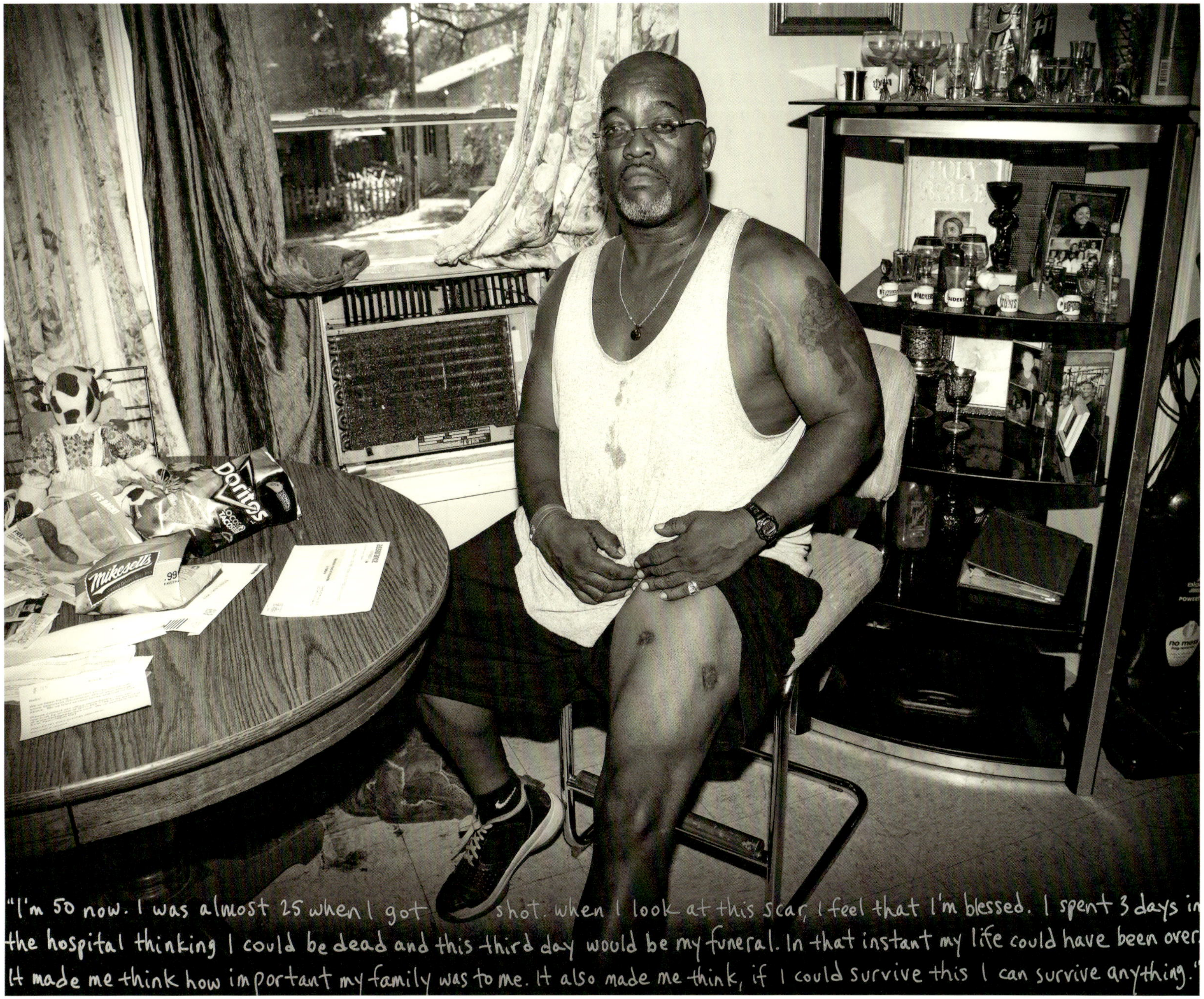

Kevin is Healed, Pigeon Hill, 2013

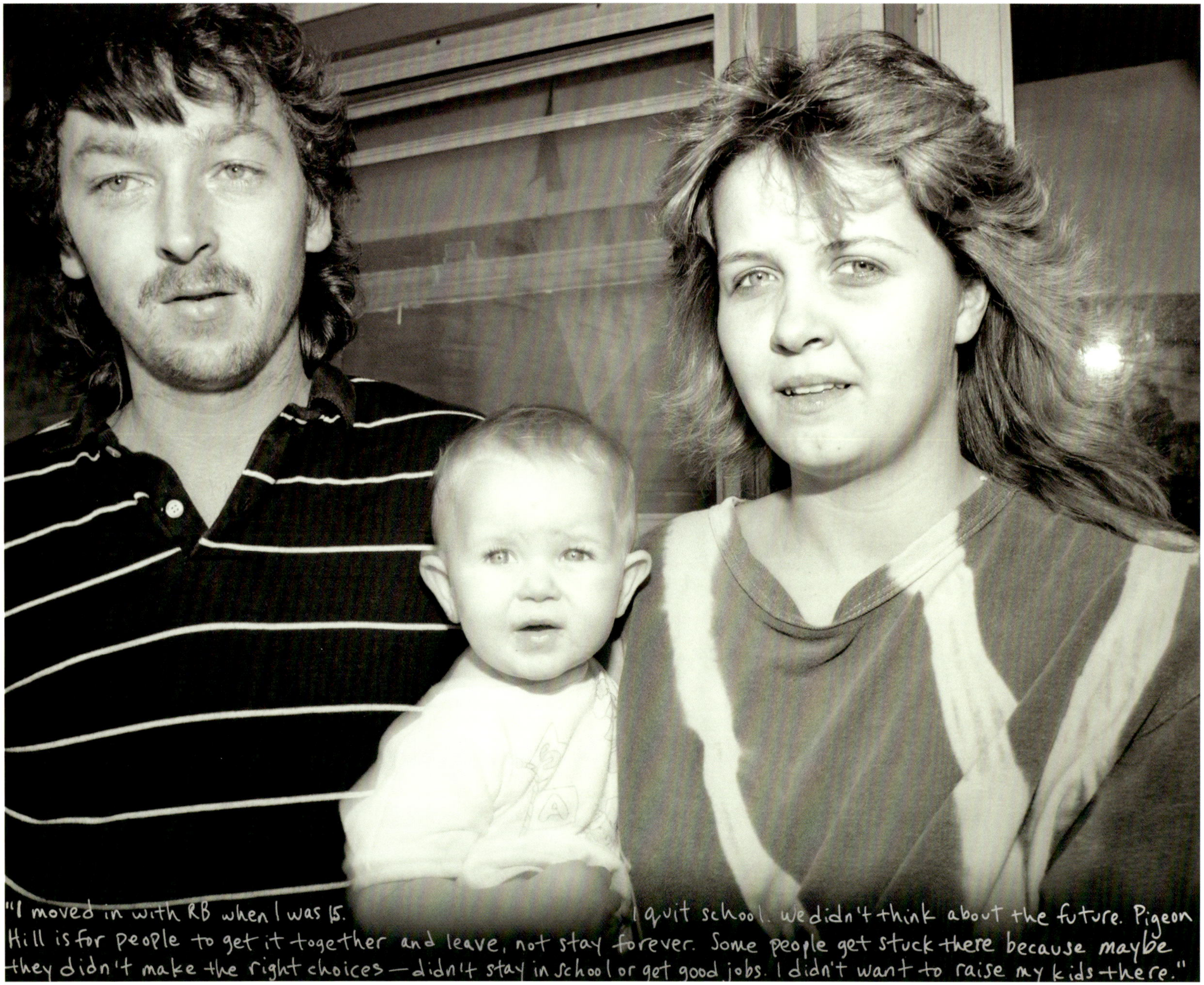

Tracy, RB, and Alyssa, Pigeon Hill, 1990

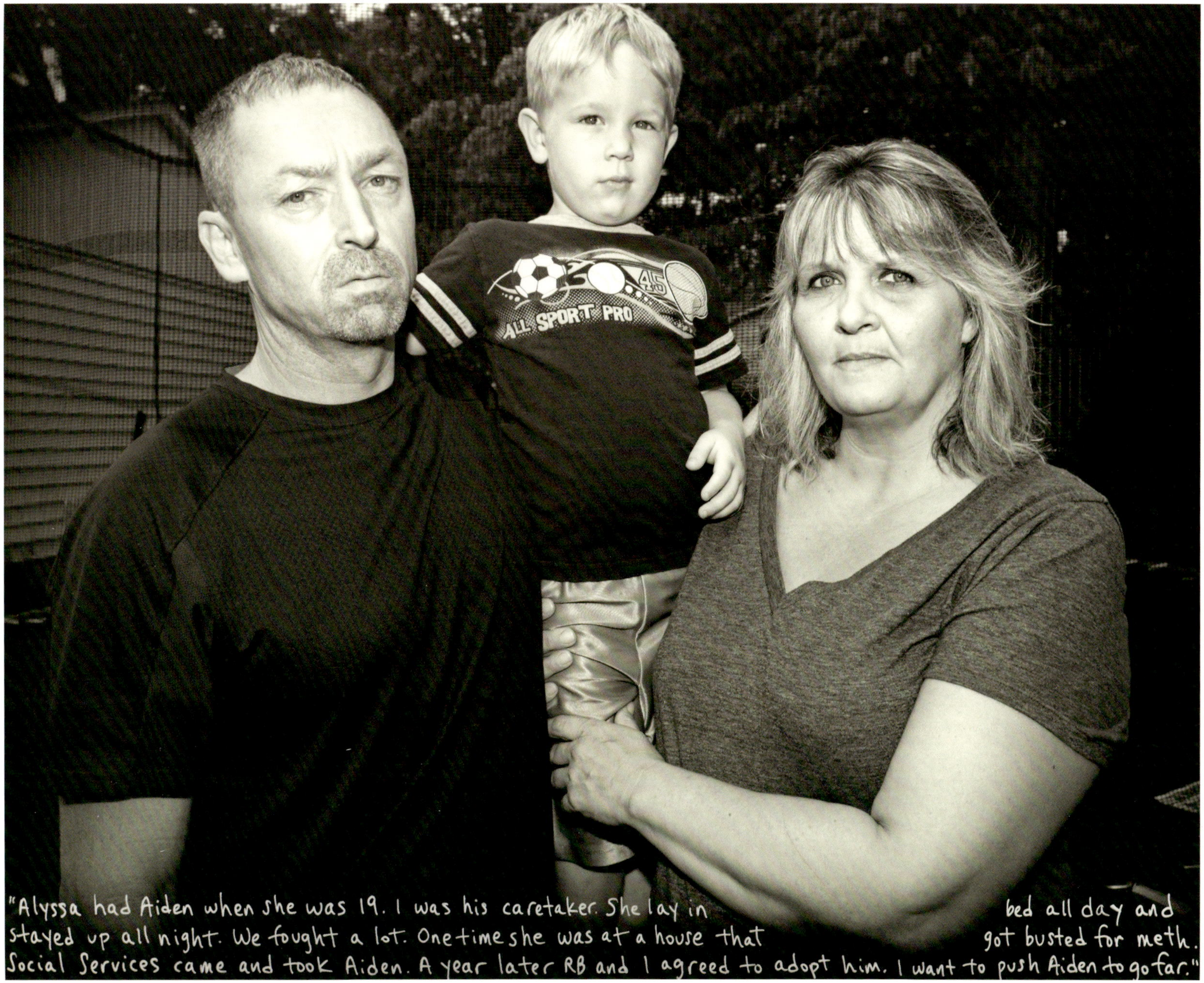

Tracy, RB, and Aiden, Ellettsville, 2013

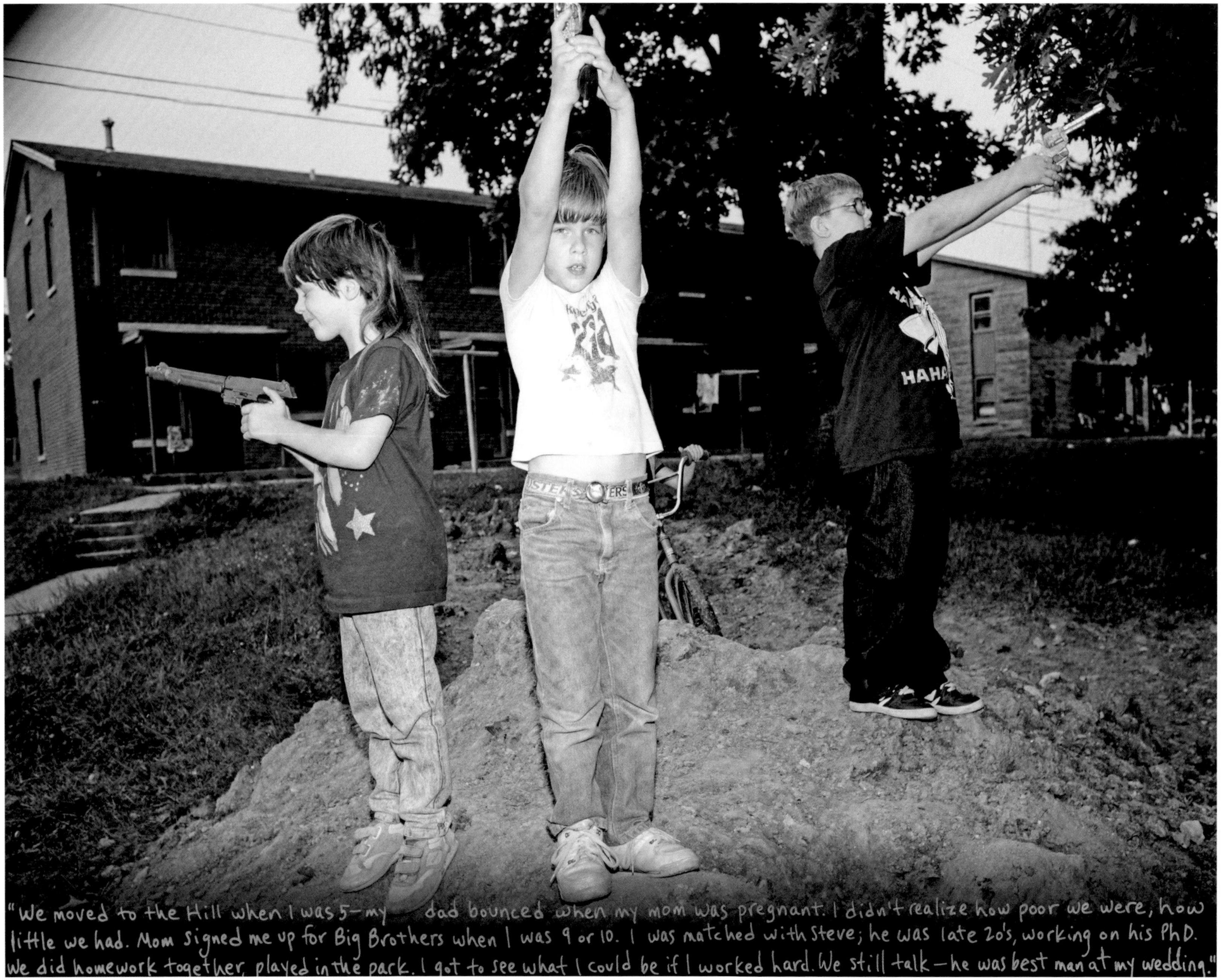

Josh Playing Cops & Robbers, Pigeon Hill, 1989

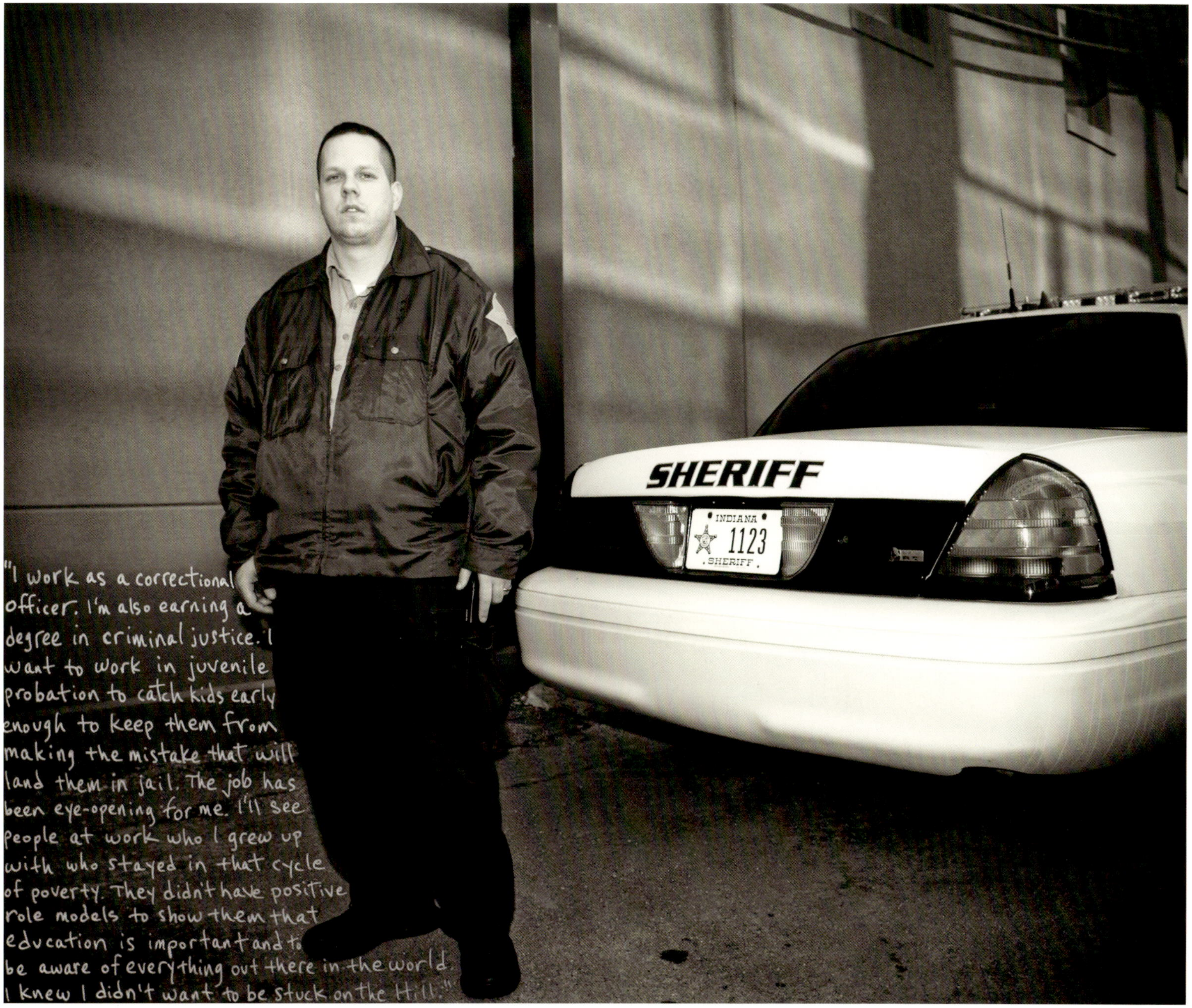

Josh, Monroe County Jail, 2016

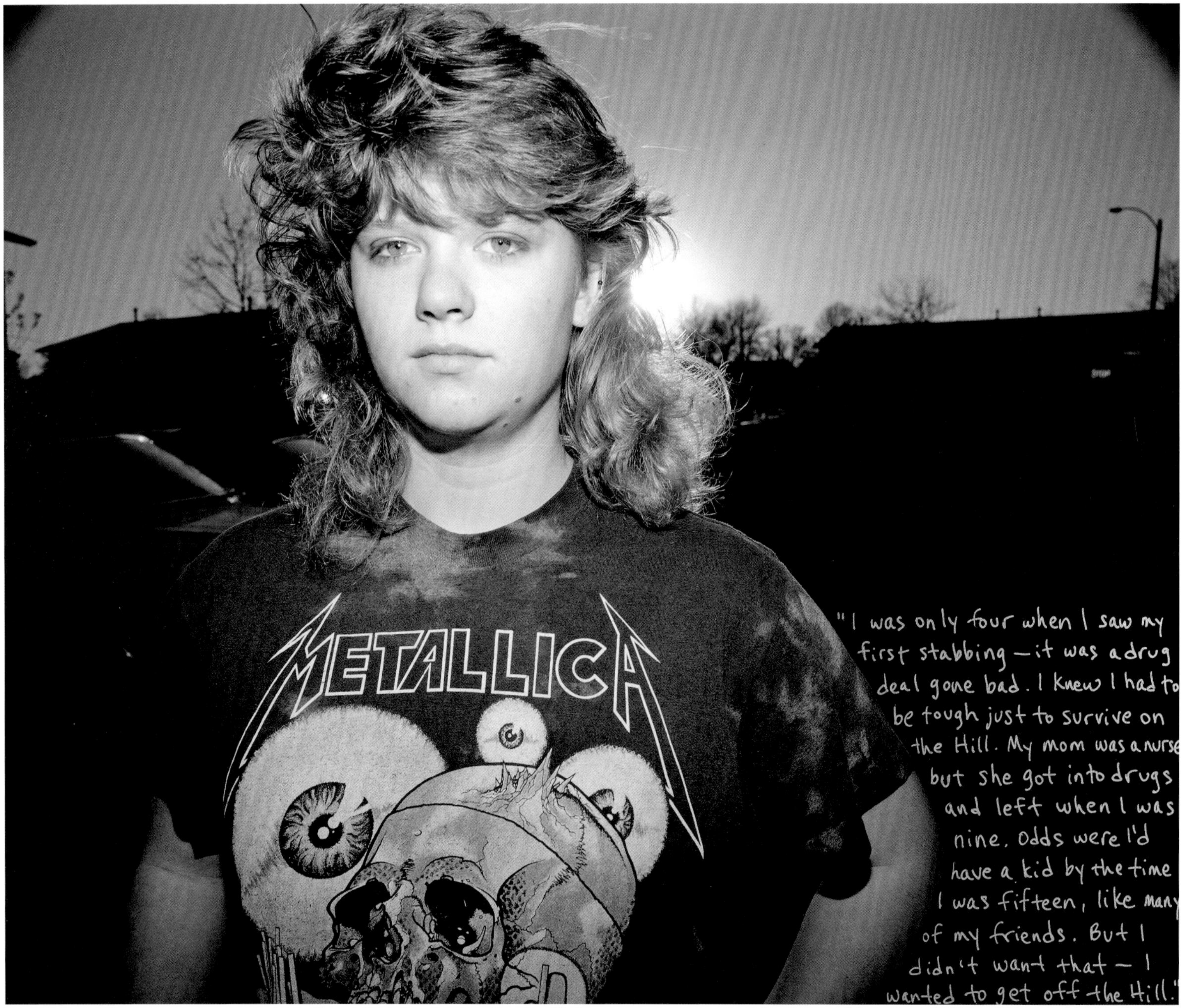

Wendi on Illinois Circle, Pigeon Hill, 1990

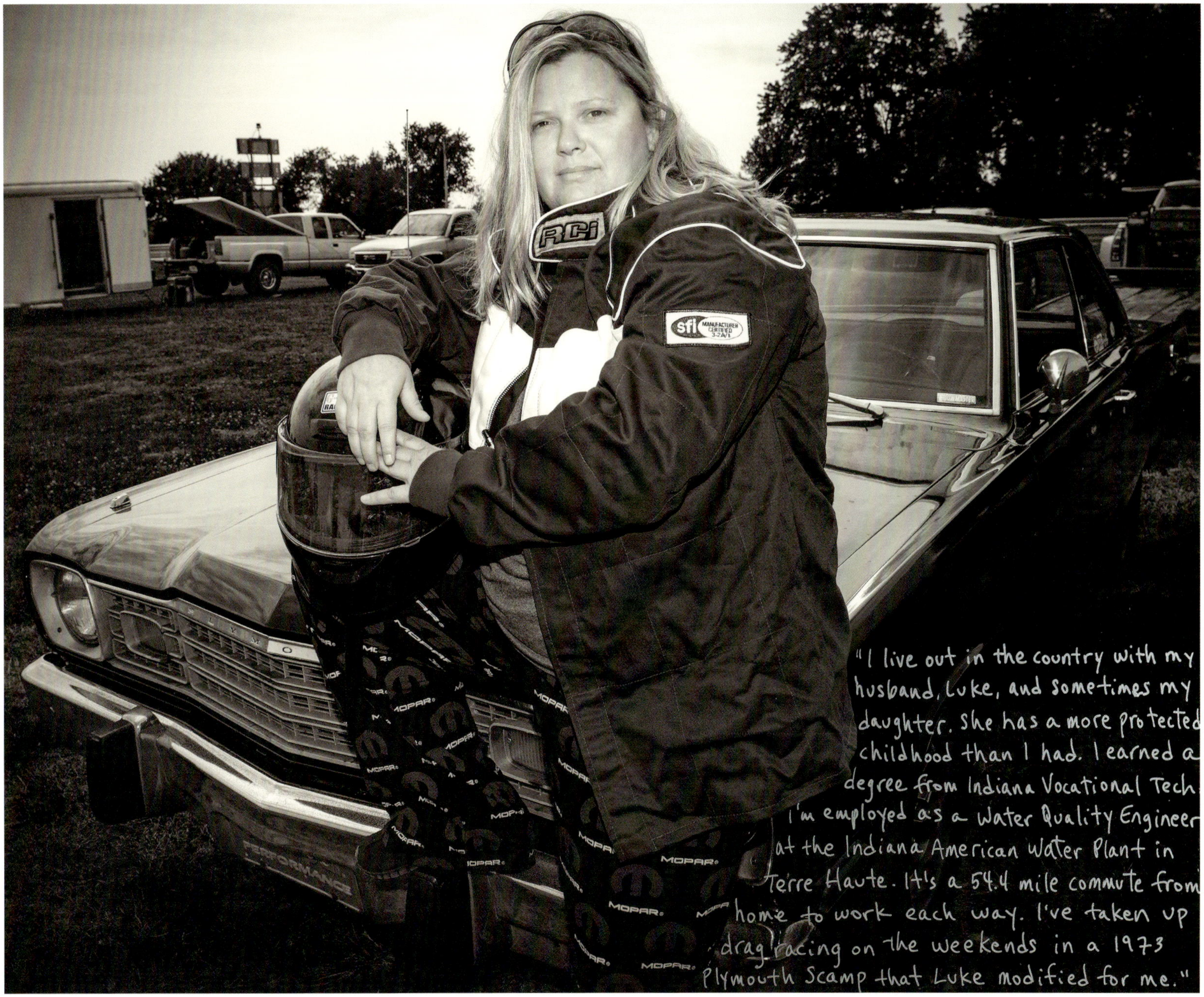

Wendi at Lyons Raceway, 2013

NOW

Photographs 2011–2015

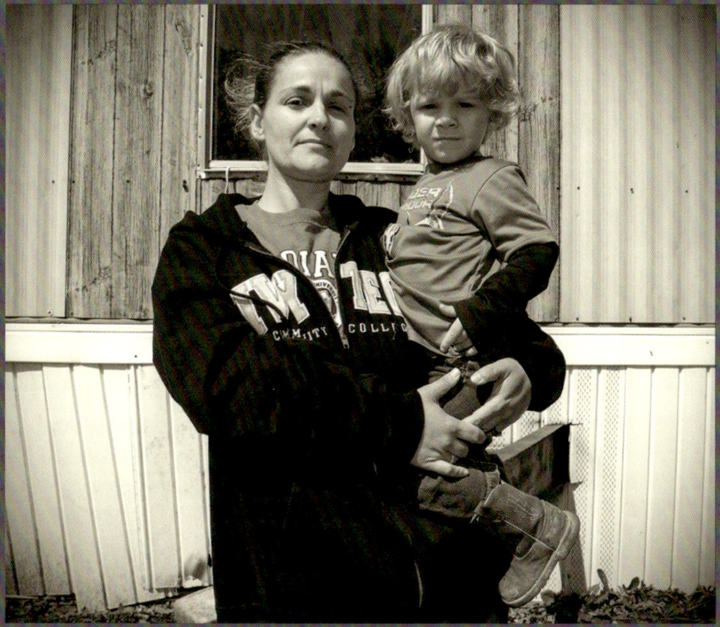

Although the portraits in this suite have no narrative written on them, many of these individuals are included in the "Then" section, while some weren't even born yet by 1991, when I took a twenty-year hiatus from photographing the residents of Crestmont. I thought it was important to include some of these singular images of past and present to provide more texture and background for the "Then & Now" pairs.

– ***Jeffrey A. Wolin***

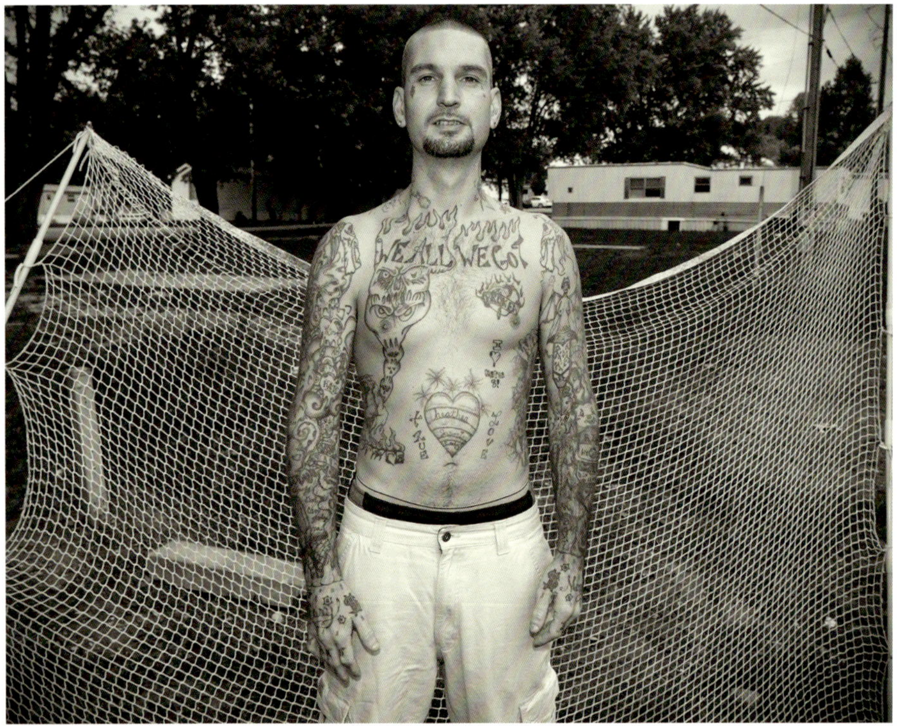
WE ALL WE GOT

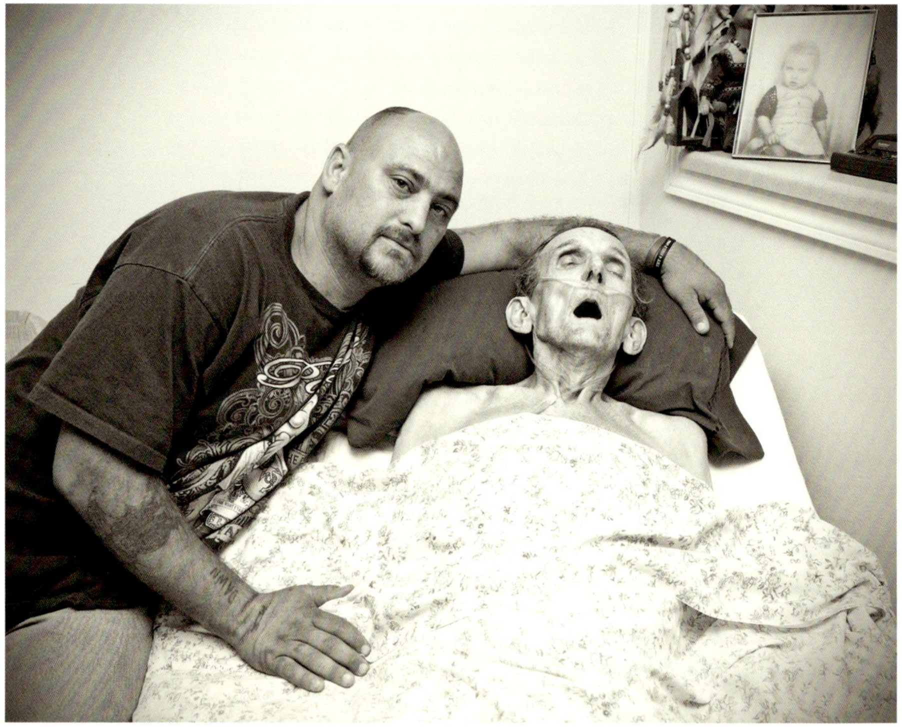

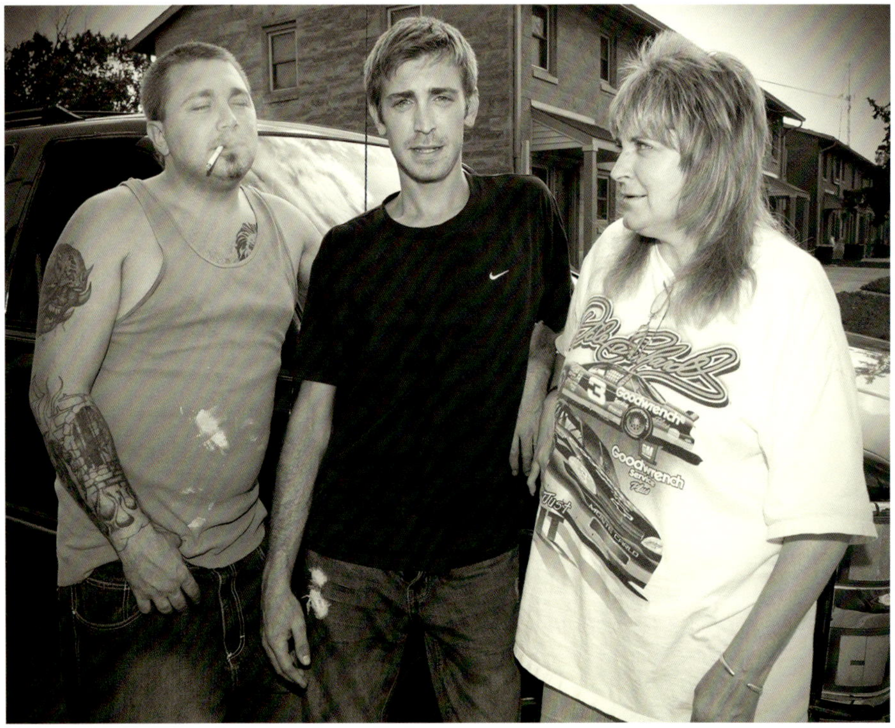
Goodwrench
Goodwrench

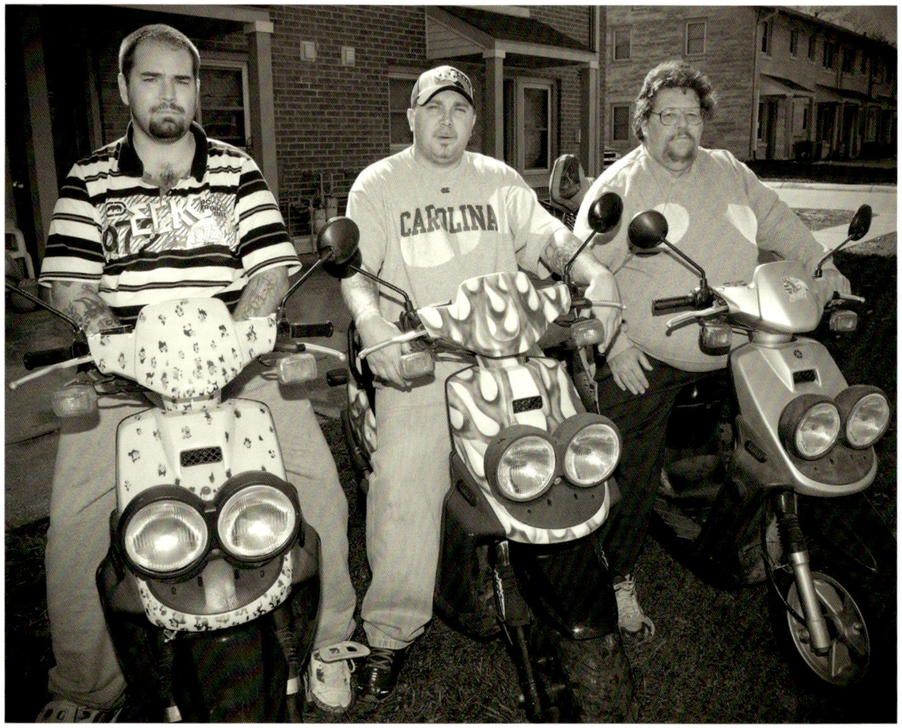
CAROLINA

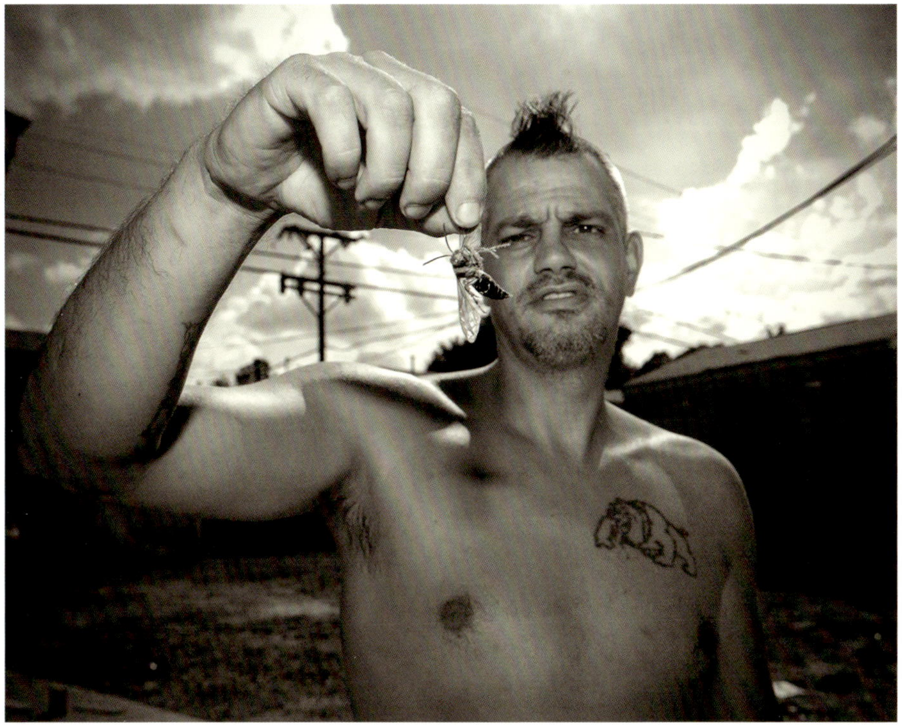

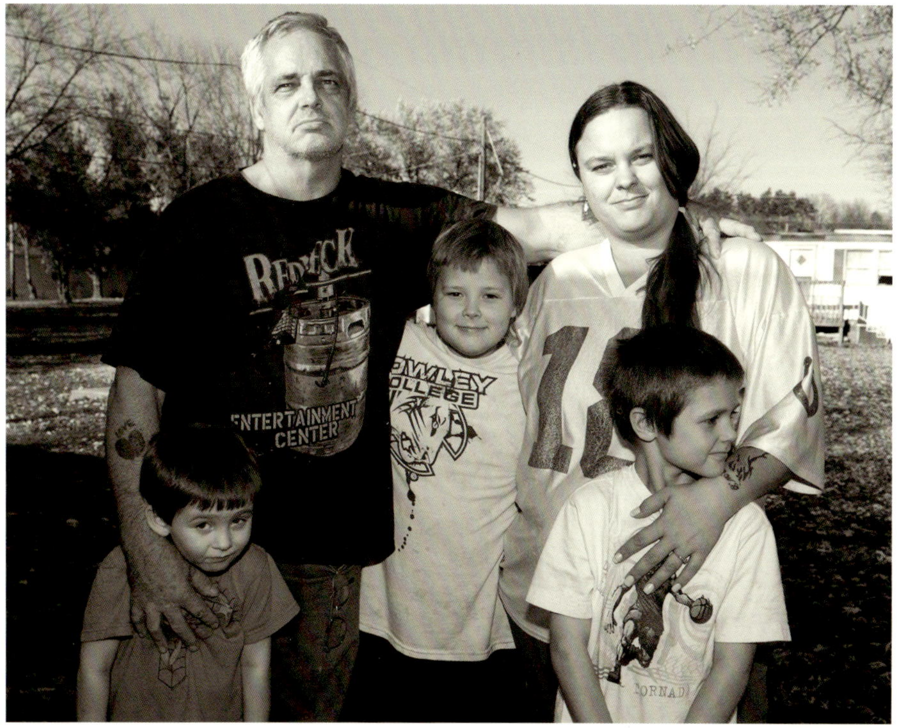
ENTERTAINMENT
CENTER

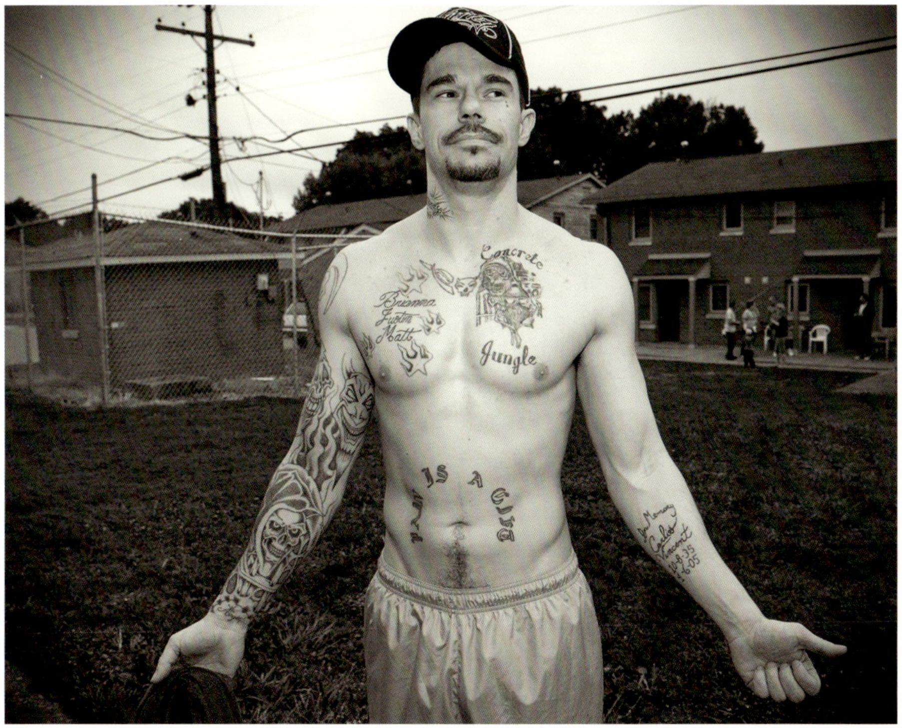
Concrete
Jungle

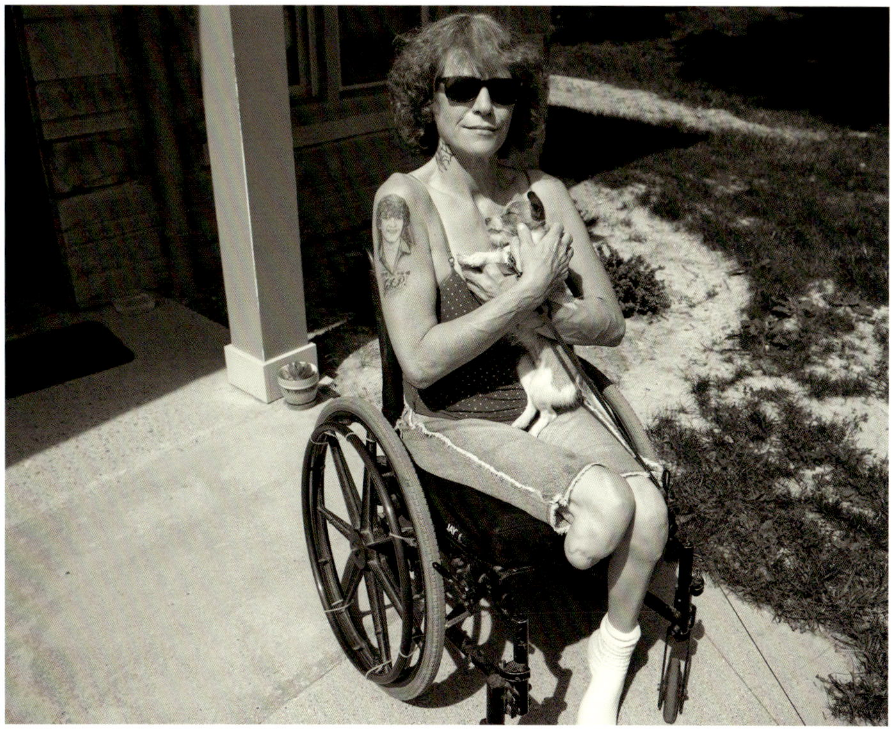

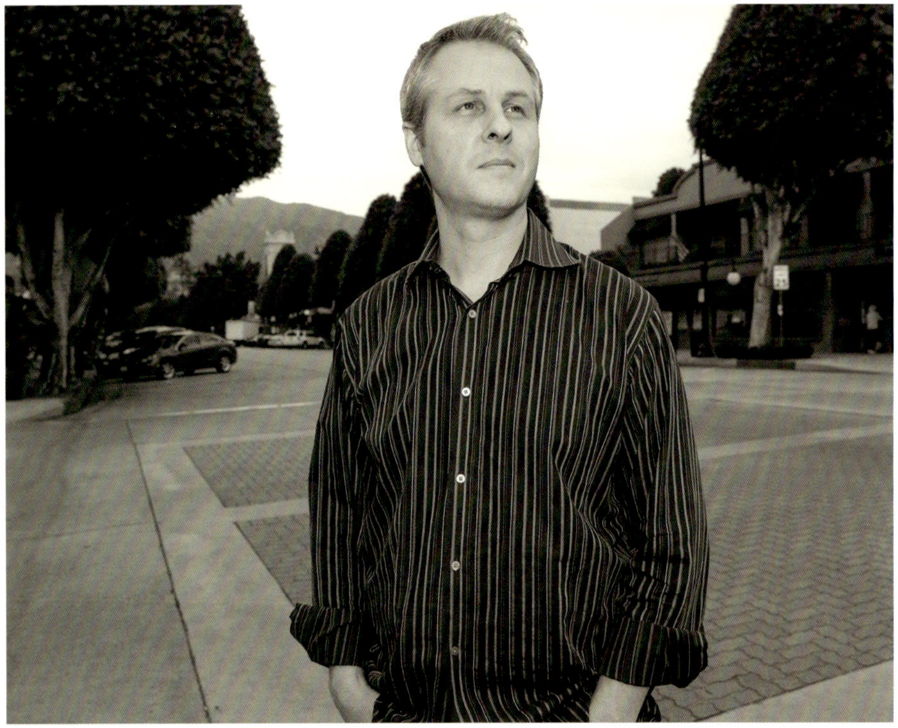

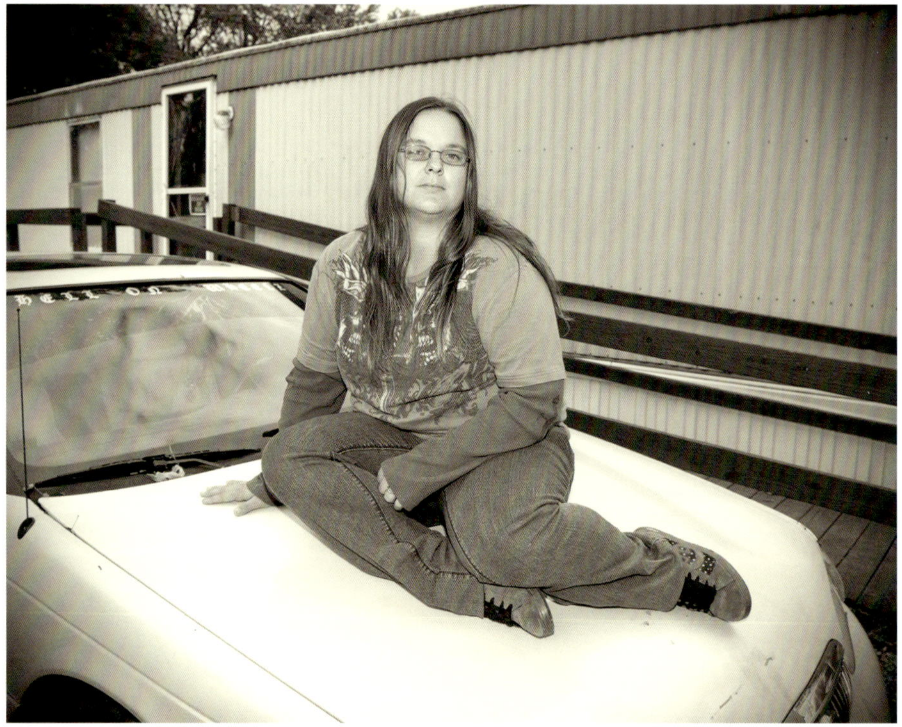

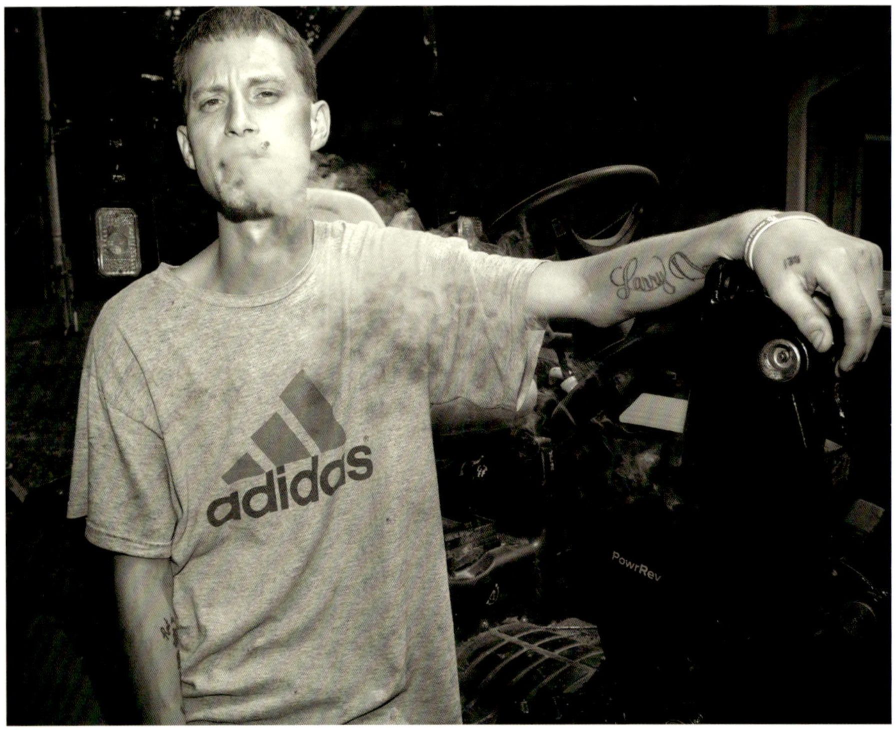

adidas
PowrRev

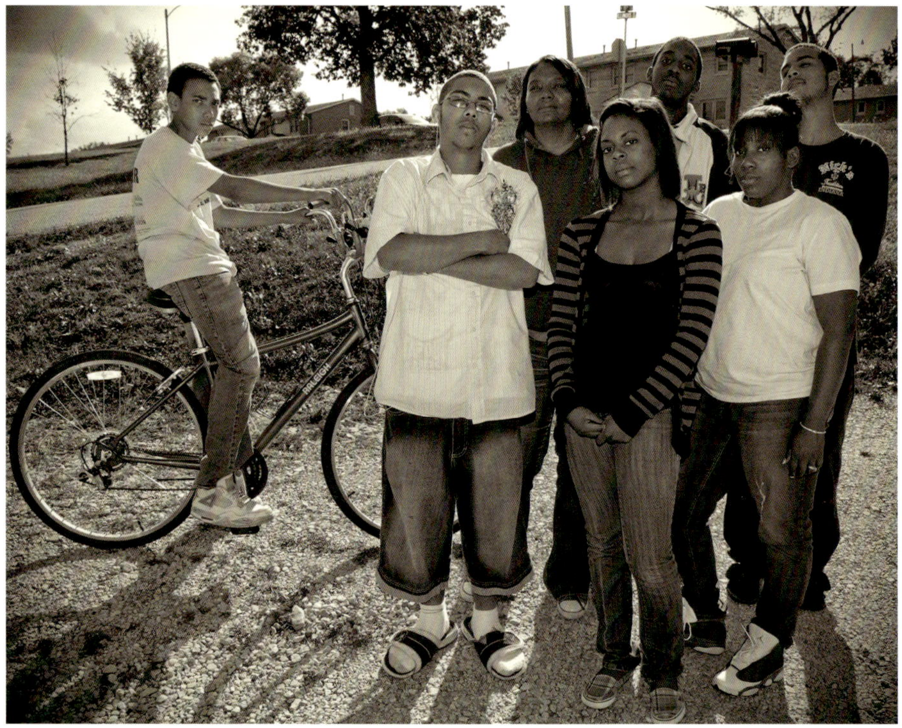

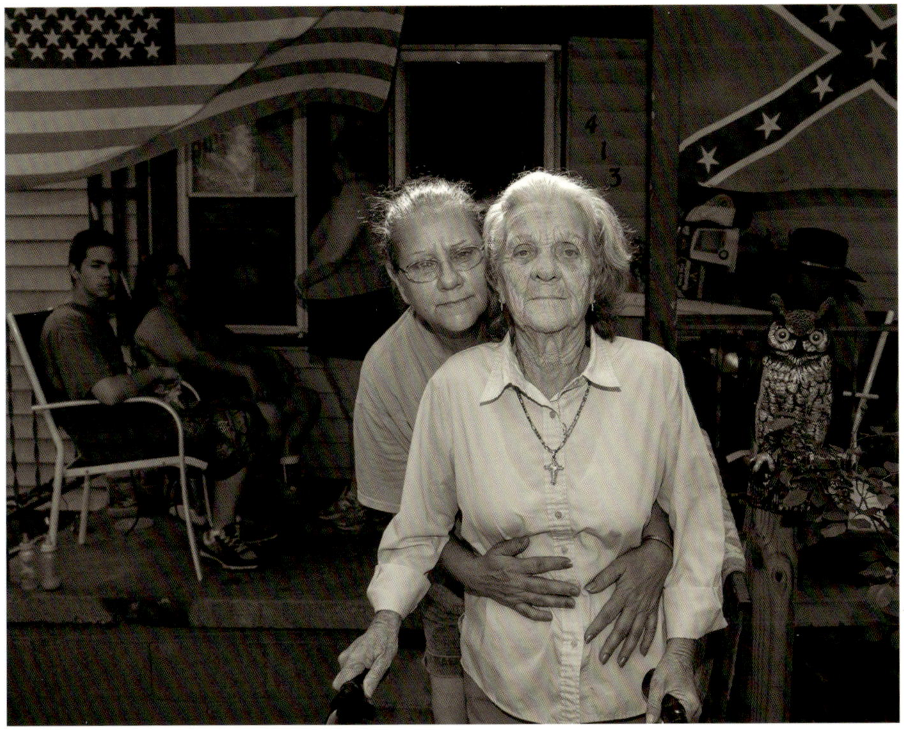
413

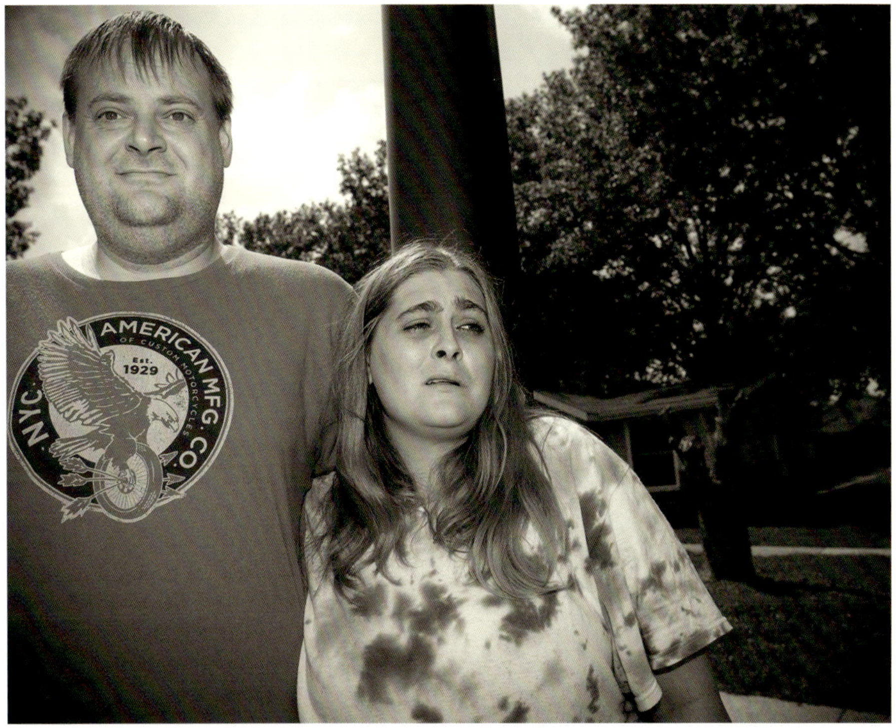
AMERICAN MFG. CO.
NYC.
Est. 1929

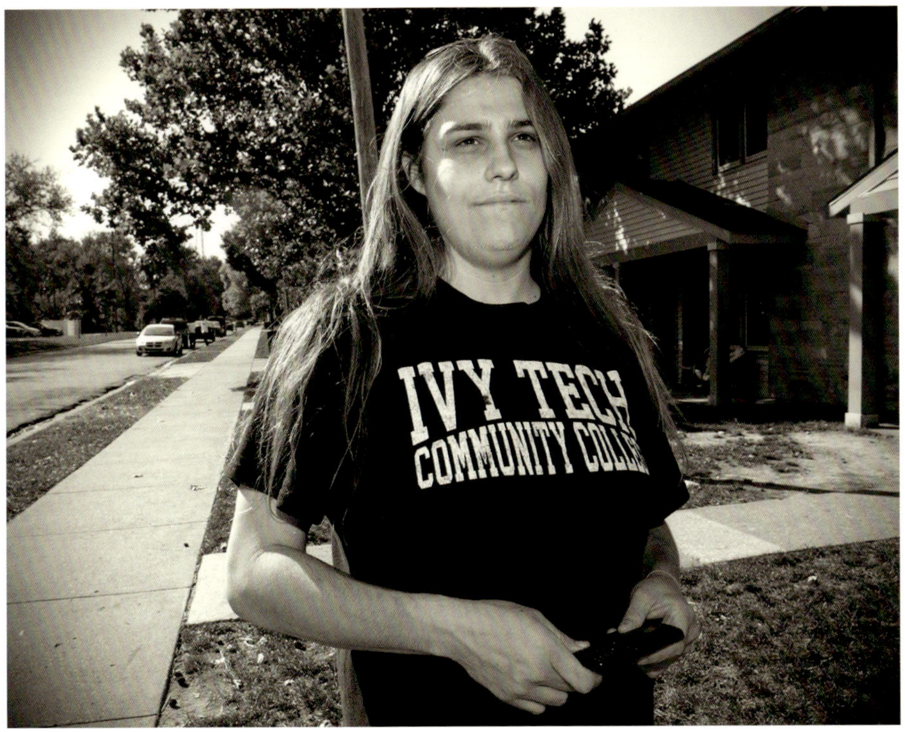
IVY TECH
COMMUNITY

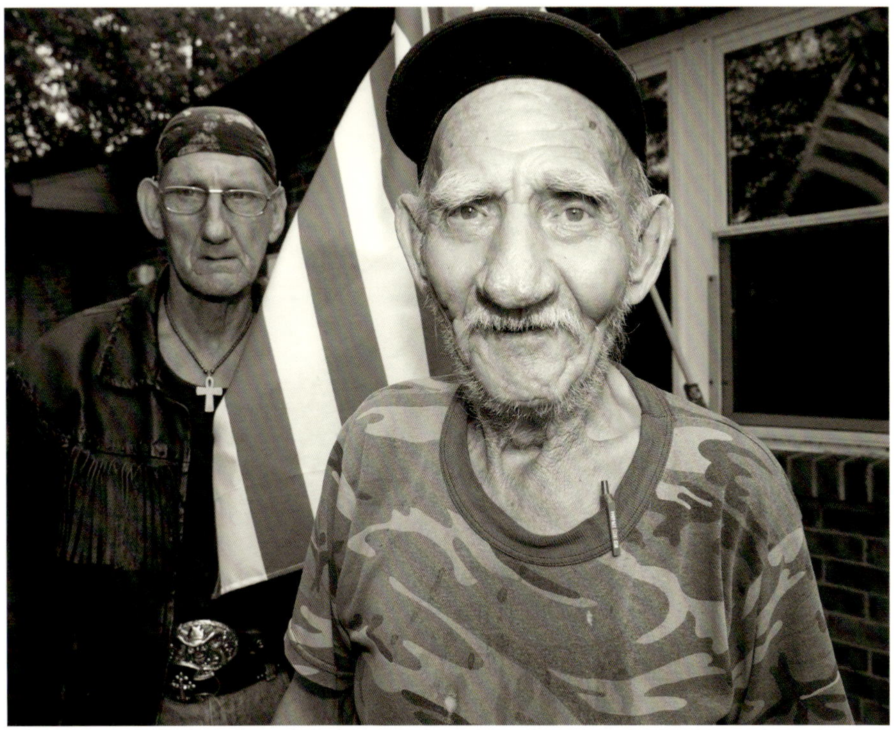

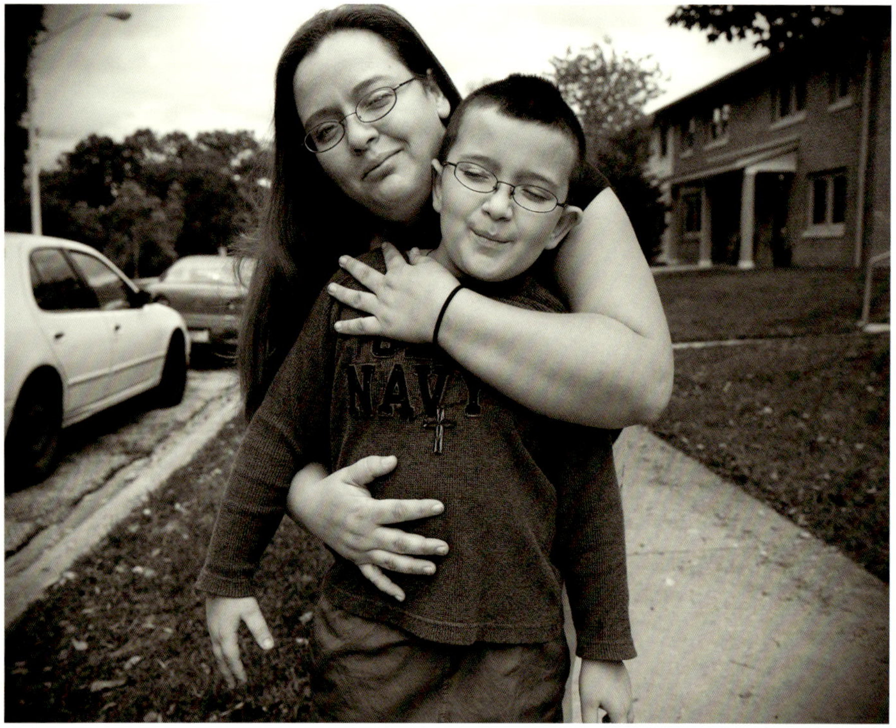
NAVY

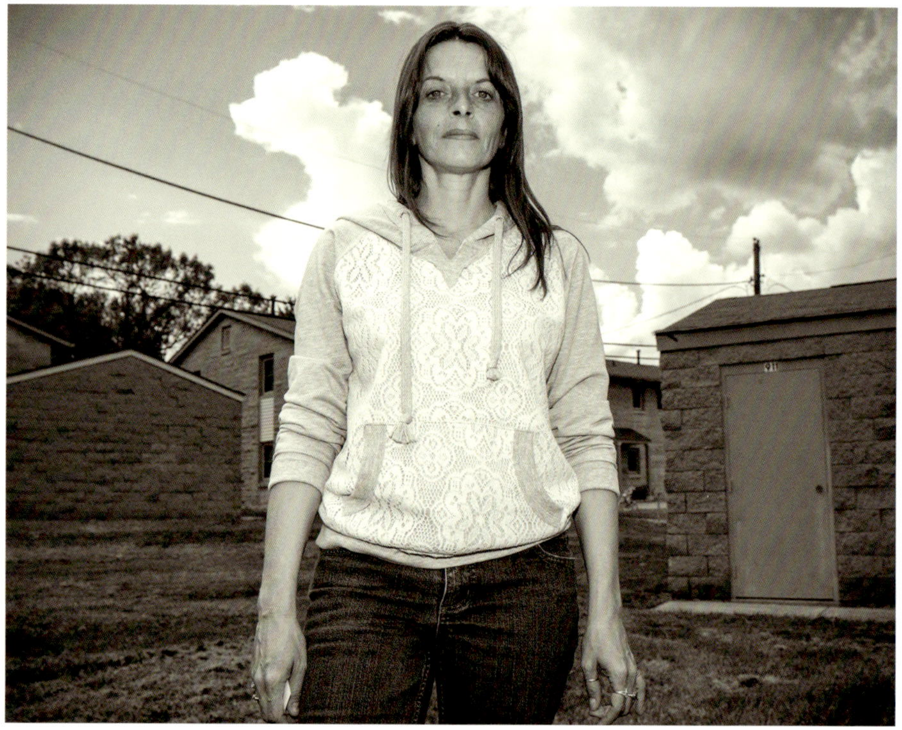

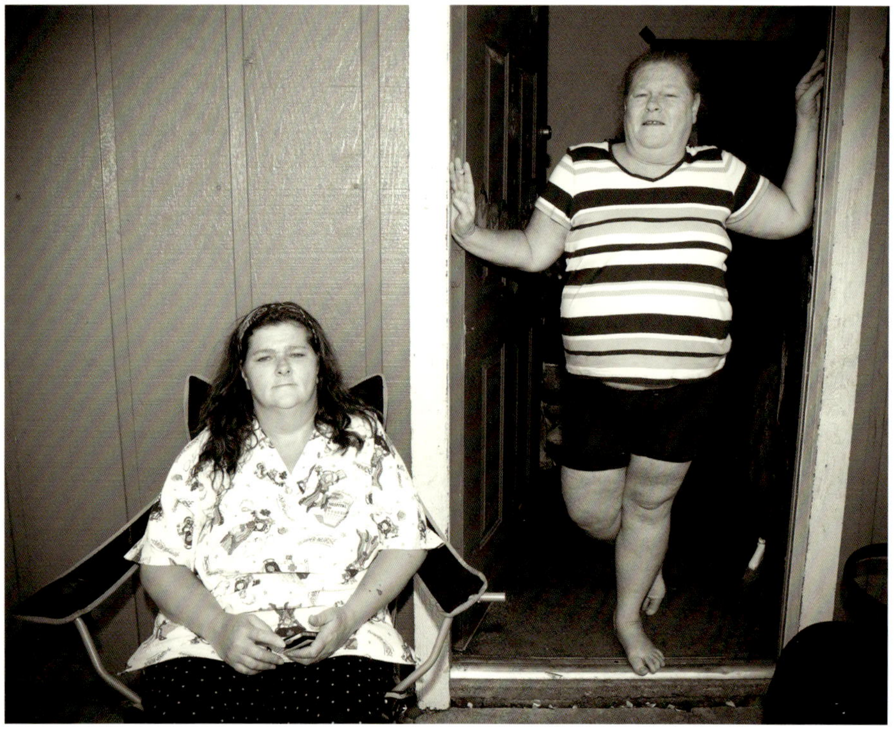

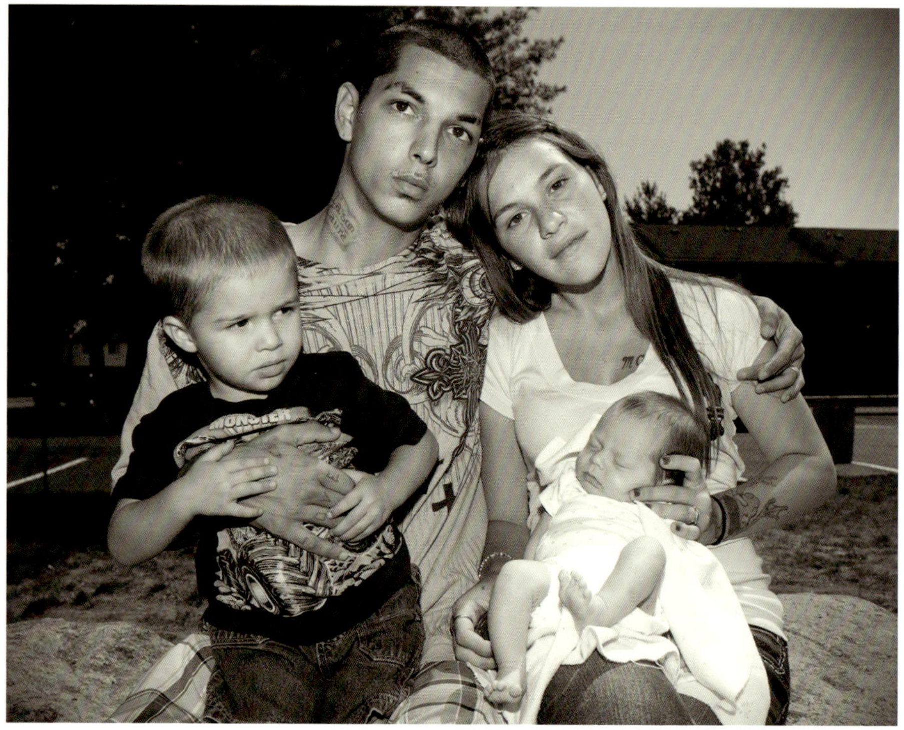

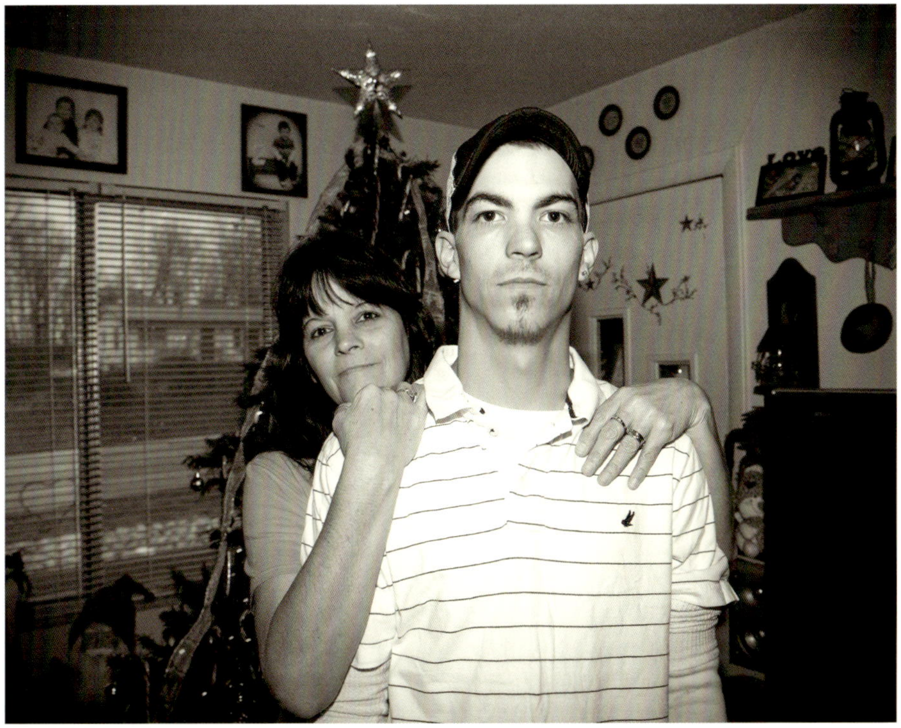
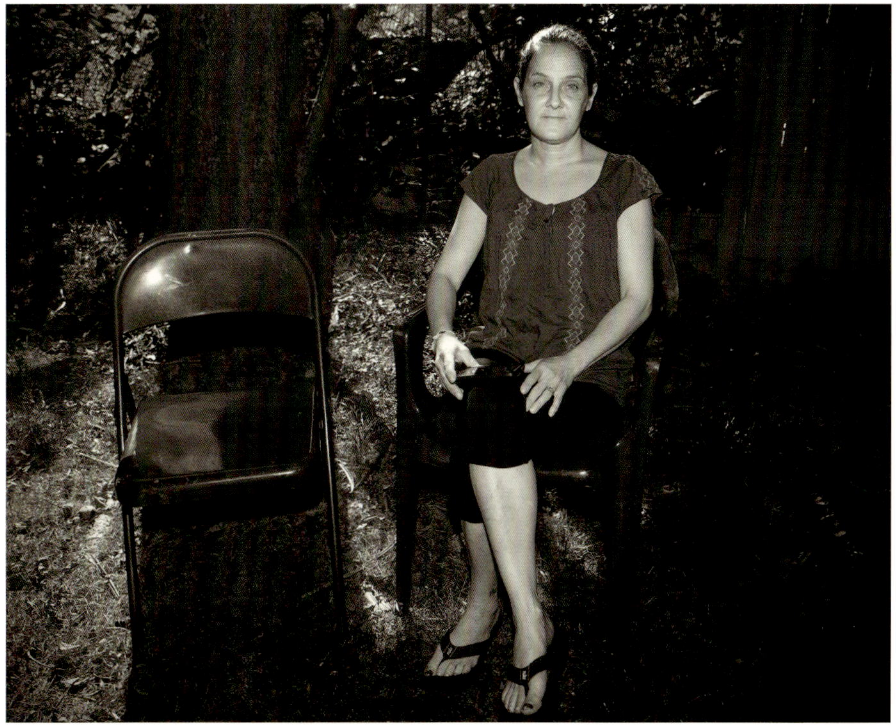
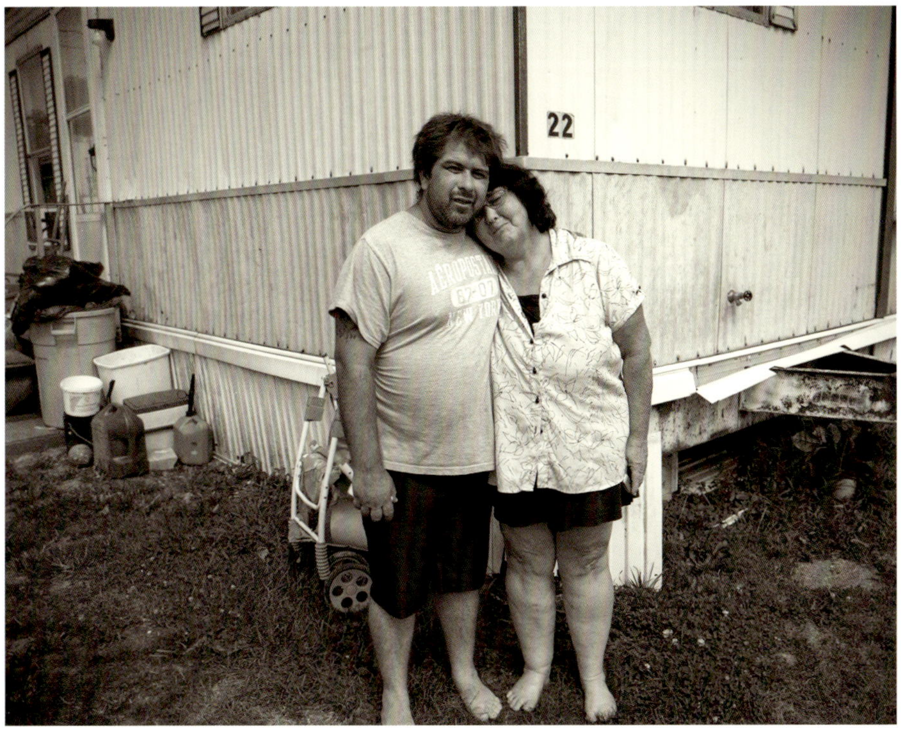
22
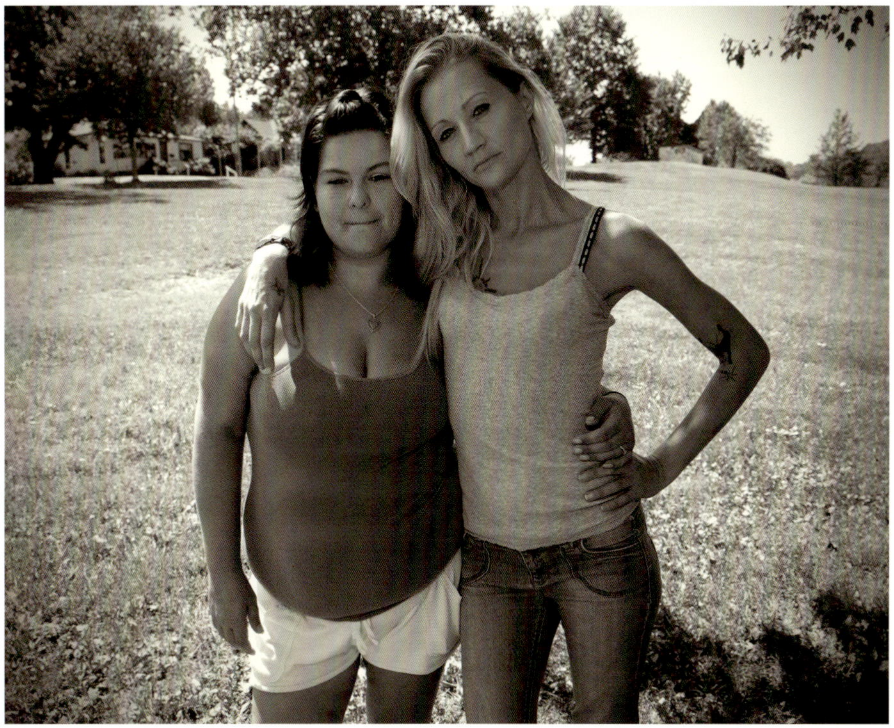

Jeffrey Wolin's work is essentially one of making portraits in which words—often handwritten on the picture—act as a detonator whose grenade is the picture. This work is occupied by memory—or, more properly, haunted by the survivors. Jeffrey Wolin's pictures are portraits and those who accept to pose for him are alive, but they all come back from "far away."

REVENANTS

Jean-Louis Poitevin

(translation from the French by Anne Hémion)

Jeffrey Wolin's work is essentially one of making portraits in which words—often handwritten on the picture—act as a detonator whose grenade is the picture. This work is occupied by memory—or, more properly, haunted by the survivors. Jeffrey Wolin's pictures are portraits and those who agree to pose for him are alive, but they all come back from "far away."

"We are the ones who create, build, impose continuity by putting these distinct unities into a stew of dreamed-time. What we see is that continuity doesn't necessarily provide meaning but that without it we are lost."

The reason why he picked these men and women lies in the fact that they carry pieces of memory that you won't find in newspapers or books, the memory of events as they have been experienced by individuals.

There is a gap that often turns into a quartering between reality as seen by the media or accredited by history and the way facts are embedded in flesh and bone. The only way to decrypt this particular memory is to admit that it is fundamentally intangible. More accurately, the only way to comprehend it is to take into account—in addition to the blinding evidence of the picture—of this rubble of pain that the human mouth spits out in the shape of words.

Voices

Each person photographed by Jeffrey Wolin has directly experienced a drama. Each individual memory is used in this series of portraits as a symbol of one of these dramas that have profoundly torn history. Diving through personal remembrances raises memories to the surface that still torment each protagonist's flesh despite the years that have elapsed. It is an attempt to make elements that could look like flesh-and-blood-colored touches on an abstract painting or on pictures from a black and white comic come to the surface—the surface of image which is also one of oblivion.

A lot of those he photographs come back from far away. They experienced the concentration camps or the war in Vietnam and survived them, but in the years that followed, the ruthless and destructive twists of fate did not spare them.

In a way, photography provides them with a body, a surface, a magic support from which their voices can be heard. We can hear them through the mediation of words they uttered, and which are most of the time handwritten on the picture they appear in. Thus, those revenants are ghosts or specters that have the ability to be heard. Nonetheless, through realistic and documentary appearances, photography renews one of its major functions, the evocation of spirits. Because beyond the personal story of these living persons, it is precisely the fact that they've become ghostly shadows of themselves that matters. And beyond their status as specters, it is the dead people they knew, who they left behind in death camps or on battlefields, who are posthumously justified through a singular being's memories.

"We should no longer see Jeffrey Wolin's photographs only as people's reflections but as reflections of reflections, reflections of specters, specters of specters, ghosts squared. And the short texts that accompany them, somehow telling us what they've become or what happened to them during these twenty years, plunge us into an irrational stupor."

Doubles
Magic and justification are two of the major functions of photography. Jeffrey Wolin uses them in order to provide recognition for a kind of memory that can hardly be found anywhere else. He works from an agnostic point of view but the intertwining and the complementarity of words and image—which we think of as two main means of communication—allow us, beyond personal beliefs, to explore these singular mental productions that paganism but mostly Christianity never stopped calling for under a mask of promises. Memory is co-essential to the picture as well as to the text.

Thus, we must look for their difference in function in order to understand the kind of system Jeffrey Wolin sets up. For sure, these "doubled" pictures he made twenty years apart and that were shown for the first time in Lyon are quite an accomplishment.

Specters and ghosts act like doubles for the beings they represent. The picture is the double of the one it shows. The text, especially when inscribed directly on the prints, makes a double out of the model—and at the same time its underside or its reverse.

In the new series about the inhabitants of Pigeon Hill, Jeffrey Wolin does not only continue a twenty-year-old project about those who live in the United States and who seem to be thrown from time immemorial into a daily struggle with violence and poverty. He brings to it a new dimension, a radical reflection about what we call time.

It is important to notice that it is the use of the "double" that makes it possible to reverse our point of view about time. This reversal implies a perspective that points out the bipolar structure of the image, which he had only shown through the use of words—the image's "other"—so far.

Stupor
This time, the entire system is split in two and simultaneously redoubled. Those who were specters as pictures and specters to American society—which, like the other developed countries, does not want to see those whose appearance and way of life don't fit into its perfect imaginary line—being photographed for the second time twenty years later, find themselves confronted with their doubles. It's as if they could see themselves or if we could see them in a mirror that were able to reflect time as well as it reflects images. They've become their own mirrors.

We should no longer see Jeffrey Wolin's photographs only as people's reflections but as reflections of reflections, reflections of specters, specters of specters, ghosts squared. And the short texts that accompany them, somehow telling us what they've become or what happened to them during these twenty years, plunge us into an irrational stupor.

Of course, one doesn't have to be a clairvoyant to know that these people had but few chances to

"Twenty years—enough time for a baby to become a man proud of his strength or for a young and attractive woman to become a woman whose face we can read like an open book in which her destiny would be written down."

escape the destiny that every society promises to those who were born into poverty. In some way, because we look them straight in the eyes, these people become the living proof of the implacable existence of a social destiny that is far from a fairy tale.

Time

Twenty years—enough time for a baby to become a man proud of his strength or for a young and attractive woman to become a woman whose face we can read like an open book in which her destiny would be written down. Enough as well for liberty to be turned into prison, or the other way around. Nonetheless, when we look at these pictures, and despite these pivotal events, which are told as briefly as a confession, it is impossible not to feel that the notion of time is in some way biased, even false. In any case, it is at least without connection to what is really experienced.

If we only look at the sociological aspect of Jeffrey Wolin's photographs, we might support the view that time is measurable and acts, in the end, as the measuring rod for everyone's life. The central illusion is obviously to think of time as a continuum, as a succession, as points that define a line, and that this line would be a text in which it would be possible to read the meaning of everyone's life.

And, paradoxically, these pictures seem to question radically this illusion. It is commonly accepted that time goes by according to the junction of individuals' personal events. But as soon as we look at the social and emotional aspects of life, time does not seem to be a homogeneous idea nor an efficient measure. In his book *Time: An Essay*, Norbert Elias shows that our vision of time is not homogeneous but bridges the gap between physical and social time:

"The construction of time theories has thus been almost exclusively the task of physicists or philosophers that acted as their interpreters. By contrast, 'social time' remained insignificant as a theme for theoretical research or, more broadly, as an object of scientific investigation. And yet its importance in men's social coexistence never stopped growing. We could even say that, by a kind of reversal of the effective course of events, it appeared as a derivative—more or less arbitrary—of 'physical time,' which is itself much more solidly structured."

Discontinuity

Jeffrey Wolin's photographs constitute a plunge into social time and an exploration of what it consists of and the nature of its very existence.

Time on clocks ticks off an infinity of instants that are supposed to make a continuous line, whereas social time is made of discontinuous elements. The power of these photographs—separated by twenty years—is to make discontinuity visible by showing adjacent instants that don't presuppose anything concerning any continuity whatsoever.

We should rather say that these pictures manage

"Jeffrey Wolin's photographs constitute a plunge into social time and an exploration of what it consists of and the nature of its very existence."

to make us put our beliefs about continuity aside, thanks to the doubling of each picture, which is at the same time explicitly simple and extremely rich in meaning.

Each pair of pictures clearly demonstrates the fact that past time, mental time, emotional time, and social time are not subordinate to physical time. Indeed, each picture represents an instant. What's important here is not to refer to the physical and technical time the photograph was taken but to the idea that each picture includes the protagonists' "voices" through the mediation of the text and that, when doubled, it makes the discontinuity of instants materially perceptible.

In a few sentences, the text abruptly reveals individual lives that only become stories because we put the two moments (then and now) together. Supposing that continuity is necessary, we are the ones who build the bridge between these two images and we call it a life story, grasping at our understanding of time.

What we see

And yet, what we see is somehow the opposite of a story. What we look at are precisely two distinct and thus discontinuous events, two disparate instants whose only connection is the rigidity of social bounds as created by a "social point of view." What we see are the stigmata left on the branded flesh of those who used to be outcasts. What we see is destiny hesitating, even though it looks like it has subordinated these bodies. Seemingly insisting on the protagonists' identities, these pictures show that nothing is possible except what's already inscribed in people's flesh by the social context they were born in. Life followed a path that is not carried by time but by its absence, at least as a power of transformation. What we see is the "self-ghost" through the ghost of the other. What we see is the "non-truth" of time as a vector of orientation. What takes place in front of us is existence demonstrating its power of inscription and destruction, both of which exist outside regular forms of time. What we see is time—time as a distance—as destruction and a new dimension of existence—a dimension strictly psychological and independent from real-life conditions in which life builds itself up and destroys itself at the same time. What we see is something quite new—the idea that dreams are not motion pictures but a succession of still images. We are the ones who create, build, impose continuity by putting these distinct unities into a stew of dreamed-time. What we see is that continuity doesn't necessarily provide meaning but that without it we are lost. What we see is life when we look at it discontinuously. What we see is the tempest of eternity striking earth like a plague of locusts. What we see is the impossibility of deciding whether we are dead or alive. What we see is that "We are such stuff as dreams are made on, and our little life is rounded with a sleep" (W. Shakespeare, *The Tempest*, Act 4, Scene I).

(Published originally in *TK-21*)

Artist Statement

Jeffrey A. Wolin

Pigeon Hill Portraits: Then and Now

From 1987–1991, using a medium format film camera I made over 2500 portraits of the residents of Bloomington's Crestmont housing projects, an area on the west side known as "Pigeon Hill." At the time, there was much discussion among politicians and the media about the problems of the welfare state and with crime and drug abuse (the crack epidemic was in full swing) and enduring poverty.

After receiving a Guggenheim Fellowship in 1991, I moved on to two other series which occupied most of the next 20 years of my work: "Written in Memory: Portraits of the Holocaust" and "From All Sides: Portraits of American and Vietnamese War Veterans." I have a strong interest in memory and trauma and much of my work involves the inclusion of text and image.

In fall 2010, a woman was murdered in Bloomington and her picture appeared on the front page of the local newspaper. I immediately recognized her as the subject of several of my portraits from many years ago and tried to find out more about her life and death by speaking with her relatives. I realized then that I wanted to locate the residents of the projects that I had photographed earlier and re-photograph them and learn more about how their lives were going, a full generation later.

At first it proved difficult to find former subjects. To aid in this process and to pay back the community for allowing me into their lives 20 years earlier, I taught a photography class to kids at the local Boys and Girls Club. After class I would wander through the neighborhood with a box of portraits from 20+ years earlier, asking everyone I met if they could identify any of the faces. Eventually I found one of the people I had photographed years ago—it was eerie and thrilling to finally come face to face with someone I had photographed many times in the distant past and to see how her face had changed from a teenager to that of a grown woman over the course of time.

She helped me find others I had previously photographed who in turn put me in touch with still others. Eventually I re-photographed over 100 individuals. I made over 3000 photographs, this time with a medium format digital camera. Some still reside on the Hill, while others have moved to nearby apartments or trailer parks. Unfortunately, some are deceased or in prison or moved away and couldn't be located.

The economic condition of many of these individuals remains poor, while others now live solidly middle-class lives. More than a few of the residents are firmly entrenched in the criminal justice system, usually for non-violent crimes such as lack of payment of child support or drug use—America has the highest incarceration rate of any country in the world. Although these issues are addressed in this series, my main interest is in the faces themselves, especially when juxtaposed with the earlier portraits. One can see the effects of the passing of time and the ways in which life's experiences (good and bad) are written into these open and expressive faces.

Acknowledgements

Acknowledgements
I would like to thank the following individuals for their help and support during the two periods when the photographs for *Pigeon Hill: Then & Now* were made: Catherine Edelman of Catherine Edelman Gallery, Chicago, who showed both the original series when it was new and the combined then and now photographs. Her wise counsel helped guide me over the years as the project took shape. Gilles Verneret, Director of la Galerie le Bleu du Ciel in Lyon, was the first to show the Then & Now series together. Keith Davis, Senior Curator of Photography at the Nelson Atkins Museum of Art in Kansas City, who wrote the insightful introduction and whose friendship and advice since our days together at George Eastman House has been much appreciated. Jean-Louis Poitevin for his profound afterword, originally published in the journal, *TK-21*.

I am grateful to Jenny El-Shamy who masterfully designed this complicated book and to the design and editorial teams at Kehrer Verlag who made the book a reality.

Other individuals and institutions whose timely support was essential for the success of this project:

David and Martha Moore of Pictura Gallery in Bloomington; Crestmont Boys & Girls Club; Museum of Contemporary Photography, Chicago; Indiana University College of Arts & Sciences for awarding me a Ruth N. Halls Professorship; the National Endowment for the Arts and John Simon Guggenheim Memorial Foundation for granting me fellowships at critical periods of my career; Peter Galassi, Director of Photography at MoMA, the first curator to acquire and show work from this series.

I especially wish to thank all the current and former residents of Crestmont housing projects on Pigeon Hill who shared with me their faces and intimate life stories.

Biography

Jeffrey A. Wolin is Ruth N. Halls Professor Emeritus of Photography at Indiana University. Wolin's photographs have been exhibited in over 75 solo and group shows in the US and Europe since 1990 including solo exhibitions at the Art Institute of Chicago, International Center of Photography in New York and the Museum of Contemporary Photography in Chicago.

His photographs are in the permanent collections of numerous museums including the Metropolitan Museum of Art, New York; Los Angeles County Museum of Art; San Francisco Museum of Modern Art; Nelson-Atkins Museum of Art, Kansas City; Cleveland Museum of Art; Houston Museum of Fine Arts; Art Institute of Chicago; New York Public Library, New York; George Eastman Museum, Rochester; Whitney Museum of American Art, New York; Bibliotèque Nationale de France, Paris; and Museum of Modern Art, New York.

Wolin's work is included in numerous monographs including *Written in Memory: Portraits of the Holocaust*, published by Chronicle Books and *Inconvenient Stories: Vietnam War Veterans* by Umbrage Editions. Other publications include *Swimmers*, Aperture, New York; *Waterproof*, Editions Stemmle, Zurich; *An American Century of Photography*, Abrams, New York; *Searching for Memory*, Basic Books, New York; *Common Ground*, Merrell, London & New York; and *Mémoire des Camps*, Editions Marval, Paris.

Wolin is the recipient of two Visual Artist Fellowships from the National Endowment for the Arts and a Guggenheim Fellowship. He is represented by Catherine Edelman Gallery in Chicago.

Texts: Keith F. Davis, Jean-Louis Poitevin, Jeffrey A. Wolin
Design: Jenny El-Shamy Design
Image Processing: Kehrer Design Heidelberg (René Henoch)
Production: Kehrer Design Heidelberg (Andreas Schubert)
Cover Illustration: *Wendi on Illinois Circle, Pigeon Hill,* 1990
Back Cover Illustration: *Wendi at Lyons Raceway, 2013*

Bibliographic information published by the Deutsche Nationalbibliothek: The Deutsche Nationalbibliothek lists this publication in the Deutsche Nationalbibliografie; detailed bibliographic data is available on the Internet at http://dnb.dnb.de.

Printed and bound in Germany

ISBN 978-3-86828-721-9

Kehrer Heidelberg Berlin
www.kehrerverlag.com